MINDFUL RELATIONSHIP HABITS

25 PRACTICES FOR COUPLES TO ENHANCE INTIMACY, NURTURE CLOSENESS, AND GROW A DEEPER CONNECTION

S.J. SCOTT AND BARRIE DAVENPORT

ISBN-13: 978-1-9835-0794-6

ISBN-10: 1983507946

Disclaimer

No part of this publication may be reproduced or transmitted in any form or by any means, mechanical or electronic, including photocopying or recording, or by any information storage and retrieval system, or transmitted by email without permission in writing from the publisher.

While all attempts have been made to verify the information provided in this publication, neither the author nor the publisher assumes any responsibility for errors, omissions, or contrary interpretations of the subject matter herein.

This book is for entertainment purposes only. The views expressed are those of the author alone, and should not be taken as expert instruction or commands. The reader is responsible for his or her own actions.

Adherence to all applicable laws and regulations, including international, federal, state, and local governing professional licensing, business practices, advertising, and all other aspects of doing business in the US, Canada, or any other jurisdiction is the sole responsibility of the purchaser or reader.

Neither the author nor the publisher assumes any responsibility or liability whatsoever on the behalf of the purchaser or reader of these materials.

Any perceived slight of any individual or organization is purely unintentional.

Contents

Your Free Gift

As a way of saying thanks for your purchase, we're offering a free companion website that's exclusive to readers of *Mindful Relationship Habits*.

With the companion website, you'll discover a collection of printable checklists, worksheets, and bonus videos. Go to the URL below to get free instant access.

Go here to Access the Mindful Relationship Habits Companion Website

www.developgoodhabits.com/mrh-website

Introduction

Before you read further, mentally project yourself back to the first months of dating your current spouse or partner. Take a minute to think about how thrilling and intoxicating it felt to begin this relationship.

It was an exhilarating time, right?

You were deeply infatuated, maybe already in love, and everything felt so easy and natural. When you were with your partner, you were fully present in the moment. Everything around you seemed to fade into the background, as you had eyes only for one another.

You found one another so insanely interesting and desirable that you'd move heaven and earth to be together as often as possible. Your lover could do no wrong, and you were inspired to put your best foot forward, to show your shiniest self in all your blazing glory.

You may have even surprised yourself by your sudden eagerness to lose those extra ten pounds and get in shape. You finally started tidying your apartment so your lover wouldn't think you were a slob. Or you gave up smoking, started wearing nicer underwear, or developed a keen interest in your partner's favorite hobby—all because you wanted to impress him or her and show how committed you were to this new connection.

Unsavory habits that were once firmly entrenched in your life miraculously loosened the vise grip on your willpower and motivation. The mere thought of your partner was enough to light a fire under you to be a better man or woman.

Any past inertia about acting on goals and projects gave way to a newfound momentum to make things happen in your life—things that your partner would find appealing and attractive.

The Power of Love

New love is so powerful that it can inspire you to do things you never thought possible—to become a version of yourself you almost don't recognize. It is a force to be reckoned with, one that very few other interests or emotions can match.

If only this "new love superpower" could be bottled. If only it lasted a lifetime instead of a few months. If only we could return at will to those initial feelings of euphoria and energy that compelled us to move mountains.

Let's fast-forward now to the present day. Maybe it's five, ten, twenty, or even fifty years since you first started dating. You and your partner love one another, but that initial infatuation has faded. The thrill has been replaced by distraction, routine, and maybe some inattention or apathy.

Old bad habits have crept back into your lives, and new not-so-positive habits have developed in the way you interact and communicate with each other. You find yourselves more easily pulled away from each other to focus on kids, work, hobbies, television, social media, and other distractions.

Some of the positive, loving habits you willingly embraced in the early days—like complimenting him every day or surprising her with flowers—have fallen by the wayside.

As the years have gone by, maybe you've neglected some of the personal habits you adopted to win over your partner, like staying fit or being tidy. The almost effortless ability to be your best self has waned, and you begin to take one another and the relationship for granted. Maybe the relationship has stalled, and you're not really sure why or what to do about it.

The Mindful Relationship

Most love relationships do stall or falter after the initial infatuation phase. This is the time when irritations with your partner start to show up and your own insecurities and past wounds begin to seep through the perfect façade you present to one another in early days.

Irritations can turn into misunderstandings, hurt feelings, resentments, and full-blown arguments. We often allow anger or passive-aggressive behaviors to infect our once-intimate bond. We allow ourselves to revert to laziness or inattention with our relationships.

Where we were once laser-focused on our partner and how to make him or her happy, we are now more focused on ourselves and how we can protect our turf, nurse our wounds, and blame our partners when things turn sour.

If we remain stuck in this post-infatuation phase, our relationship can languish in a state of discontent for years, until it slowly unravels, leading to two people living separate lives.

This is not the kind of relationship we imagined for ourselves when we first got together.

You might ask yourself: How did I become so disconnected? Why do we turn away from one another? Why does the person I once thought hung the moon now push every possible button on my emotional switchboard?

Couples who find themselves stuck in a cycle of hurt feelings, blame, anger, reactivity—or simply boredom and apathy—do have a path forward. It is possible for them to find a way back to the loving, fun, sexy, intimate relationship they once shared.

It is at this stage of disconnection that couples have the greatest opportunity for personal growth and happiness—through the practice of *relationship mindfulness.*

Mindfulness simply means to pay attention, to be present, to be engaged, to be aware, to be conscious. When you apply these behaviors to your relationship, it can only grow stronger and more joyful.

As we mention in our book, *10-Minute Mindfulness*, "The more you practice mindfulness, the more present moments you'll savor and the *less unconscious* you will become. More of your actions and decisions will be grounded in awareness, allowing you to be responsive rather than reactive."

When you have a mindful relationship with your partner, you are *intentional* about all your choices and actions within it. You become more responsive to each other and less reactive to your challenges and ego needs. You evolve to a higher level of interaction with one another, one in which your focus is not so much on yourselves but more on the health, happiness, and intimacy of the relationship.

In a mindful relationship, you make conscious choices for yourself and as a couple that prioritize your close connection and minimize the possibilities for divisiveness and pain. This can be a tall order, as we all have baggage, wounds, and insecurities that can sabotage our efforts.

But when you are more intentional about your relationship, you learn skills that will help you heal the past and move forward with more self-awareness, emotional maturity, and confidence. As you both grow as individuals, your relationship will evolve past the heady intoxication of your early love to a more mature and satisfying intimacy.

Reverse Engineering Your Relationship with Mindful Habits

If the thrill of new love naturally inspires you to be attentive to your partner and more willing to develop positive habits, one must wonder if mindfully practicing these same positive behaviors now can inspire you to feel the exciting connection of new love again. Can you reverse engineer your choices and behaviors to re-create the closeness, passion, and thrill of your first months together?

Let us ask this a different way: If your partner treated you with the same love, desire, respect, attention, and tenderness he or she showed you in the beginning; if your partner practiced the same self-care and personal initiative; and if you showed these things back to your partner, would your relationship improve?

Of course, it would!

How could it not if you both were communicating easily, reigniting your chemistry, enjoying conflict-free time together, and seeing one another in the best light possible?

But is this time-travel scenario realistic? Is it even possible?

You may not be able to recapture the same exhilarating magic you experienced back in the day, but you can reignite your feelings, deepen your intimacy, and overcome your challenges more easily by choosing to have an *intentional relationship* based on the foundation you have built as a couple.

Your years together have given you gifts that are immensely valuable and satisfying—mutual comfort, devotion, security, familiarity, commitment, attachment, and shared memories.

Now, imagine having this foundation of mature love, coupled with some of the feelings you experienced early in your relationship. Imagine relearning ways to please, inspire, and love one another that reenergize your connection and bring you closer than you ever thought possible.

Use Habits to Revive Your Love

By developing or strengthening some of the relationship habits that came so naturally years ago, you can reignite old feelings and build a healthier, happier, sexier, and more mindful relationship with your partner.

Even if things have grown difficult between you, and there are challenging issues to deal with, just adopting a few new positive behaviors or dropping some negative habits can change the entire tenor of your relationship. Because you are now *paying attention with intention* to your partner and the quality of your connection, you will see a positive shift in the way you interact with one another.

The purpose of this book is to teach you how to have a more mindful relationship by applying 25 specific habits and practices. These habits will help you be more present with one another, communicate better, avoid divisive arguments, and understand and respond to one another's needs in a more loving, empathic, and conscious way.

We know the idea of "developing habits" to improve your relationship might not seem sexy or appealing. Most of us think of hard work when we think about adopting new habits and dropping bad ones. We've all been through the struggles of trying to lose weight, start an exercise routine, or declutter our homes—only to give up too soon and feel like failures.

However, there are three reasons why developing mindful *relationship* habits can be a positive and successful experience for you and your partner.

» First, unlike with other habits that can take weeks or months to see results, most of these mindful relationship habits will improve your connection and closeness right away. Even when you create a very small, positive change in your behavior, you will see immediate results with your partner. A little attention, love, kindness, respect, tenderness, compassion, and thoughtfulness go a long way.

» Second, we teach you how to develop new habits and release bad ones in a way that isn't overwhelming or difficult. Steve and Barrie are habit creation authors and experts, and they provide a template for developing habits in a way that ensures they stick for the long term. You won't have to deal with the feelings of regret and failure that come with giving up too soon. We teach you how to start small and build on your habits to ensure success.

» Finally, we firmly believe that your intimate relationship is *the* most important relationship in your life—the centerpiece of your family life, around which all other people and life endeavors revolve. A mindful, evolved relationship translates to a happy, healthy life. Knowing this, you should feel highly motivated to take care of your relationship. This motivation will keep you energized as you work on embracing new behaviors with your partner.

With the relationship habits outlined in this book, we draw from personal experience as well as from a variety of relationship and mindfulness experts and scientific research. We outline the habit, why it is so valuable to the health of your relationship, and how to implement it so that it becomes a natural part of your interactions with your partner.

If you adopt just a few of the habits in this book over the next few months, you will see a profound and positive change in your relationship. Over a year's time, you will enjoy deeper levels of love, intimacy, and happiness, which are the fruits of your long-term commitment to these mindful relationship habits.

About *Mindful Relationship Habits*

The main purpose of the following book, *Mindful Relationship Habits: 25 Practices for Couples to Enhance Intimacy, Nurture Closeness, and Grow a Deeper Connection* is to inspire you to be more intentional in your marriage or love relationship and to give you strategies for adopting positive new habits (or changing bad habits) so your relationship grows stronger, closer, and happier.

We encourage you to view your love relationship as the most precious, valuable, and important part of your life. With that mind-set, you will want to be proactive and attentive to how you take care of it and your significant other.

The habits we outline here relate to common issues couples face as well as proactive actions couples can take to protect their bond and prevent future challenges from pulling the relationship apart. Not every habit will apply to every couple.

Obviously, you won't be able to adopt every habit outlined here right away. We recommend you read through the entire book and make notes about habits that apply to your current situation or relationship goals. Then choose one habit at a time to focus on for four to six weeks or until the new behaviors feel natural and automatic. You might also want to keep a journal to document your progress and your thoughts and feelings along the way.

Some habits we outline involve several behavior changes or smaller habits. For example, Habit #2: Learn Emotional Intelligence requires adopting a series of behaviors and mind-sets. You may need to modify the work on these bigger habits by breaking them down into smaller areas of focus and action.

Of course, it's best if you and your partner read this book together and work as a team to adopt any new relationship habits. When both partners are committed to change and growth, it expedites the positive results you will see in your relationship and allows you to grow together as a couple.

If you have purchased this book on your own, invite your partner to join you in reading it, and discuss what you are learning together. Make a mutual decision that you want a mindful relationship in which you work as a team to nourish and protect your love.

When one partner is eager and willing to work on the relationship and the other partner is resistant, it makes it much more challenging to build a close and healthy connection. The resistant partner's lack of participation can impact the motivation and enthusiasm of the willing partner.

Even so, it is still well worth developing these relationship habits on your own, even if your partner doesn't participate. Your more attentive, thoughtful behaviors and words will serve as a model for the way you want your partner to respond and can motivate him or her to join you in this valuable work.

Now let's dive into the content, starting with six reasons why relationships often fall apart—and how mindfulness can help fix this issue.

6 Reasons Why Relationships Fall Apart

Before we cover mindful relationship habits and how to develop them, we believe it's valuable to first understand why relationships begin to falter and even fall apart.

With a third to a half of all marriages ending in divorce (depending on a variety of factors, such as income level, education, etc.), and with over 40% of people reporting unhappiness in their marriages, it's clear that most of us need better education about what it takes to maintain a happy relationship.

The sooner you learn how to be a more mindful partner and care for the relationship properly, the better chance you have of creating a connection that not only survives but also thrives. Young couples can save themselves years of distress by proactively taking measures to protect their relationship before the first signs of trouble erupt.

Sadly, there are no required courses in our education system teaching us how to behave and communicate in a love relationship. In fact, you must jump through more hoops to get a driver's license than you do a marriage license.

However, the *impact* of an unhappy or failed relationship has far-reaching consequences that impact a couple's long-term health and happiness, not to mention the impact it has on children, friends, and extended family. Divorce and breakups take a tremendous emotional, financial, and even physical toll on everyone involved.

Learning how to build and nurture a healthy love relationship is one of the most important endeavors you will ever undertake—maybe the most important. As we'll discuss later, a healthy marriage or committed relationship can profoundly improve all areas of your life.

Most of us learn how intimate relationships work by observing our parents. If our parents were good role models for a healthy, loving relationship, then we have an advantage in our own. If our parents were poor role models, then we are left guessing what a healthy relationship looks like and how to conduct ourselves in a marriage or love partnership.

In addition to parental influences, we bring our own preconceptions, needs, past wounds, and communication styles into our relationship, which further determines how it will progress. If we don't learn how to effectively manage the challenges, our relationships are doomed to mediocrity at best and flat out failure at worst.

There are hundreds of reasons why relationships fail, including truly devastating reasons like infidelity, abuse, and addiction. But more often than not, **relationships unravel due to lack of attention and effort**.

Years of repeated bad habits and unconsciousness add up to a slow erosion of the love and intimacy that brought you together. Good couples find themselves in a slow and painful decline because they can't seem to extricate themselves from destructive patterns, reactivity, and bad habits.

Dr. John Gottman, renowned psychologist and relationship researcher, has conducted extensive research on couples and why relationships fail. He has been able to predict whether a couple would divorce with over 90% accuracy based on six predictive factors.

Engaging repeatedly in the bad habits involved in each of these factors will assuredly lead you down a path of unhappiness and disconnection from your partner. Let's look at each of these factors and the related behaviors that can turn into destructive relationship habits.

Predictive Factor #1: Poor Conflict Communication

The way a couple communicates during times of conflict is a clear indicator of the potential success or failure of the relationship. When the conversation begins with criticism or sarcasm (which is a form of contempt), it sets the tone for the rest of the discussion.

Gottman's research shows that if a discussion begins with a harsh startup, it will nearly always end on a negative note. In fact, 96% of the time, you can predict the outcome of a discussion based on just the first three minutes. If this harsh startup is a consistent pattern, it takes a serious toll on the marriage.

Predictive Factor #2: The Devastating Four Horsemen

There are four types of negative interactions that Gottman has identified as lethal to a close and mindful relationship. He calls them the "Four Horsemen of the Apocalypse." They include criticism, contempt, defensiveness, and stonewalling, and if they are regular visitors in your relationship, they spell real trouble.

» **Criticism** is the first damaging behavior. As Barrie says in her book *Write It Out, Don't Fight It Out*, "When you criticize your partner, you are basically suggesting that their personality or character is the problem. The problem isn't the problem—your spouse is the problem." Criticism is different from making a complaint about your partner's behavior. A complaint is an issue with the behavior, not the person.

» **Contempt** reveals your feelings of superiority over your partner—as though you are looking down on his or her character or personality. It shows up as sneering, sarcasm, cynicism, eye-rolling, name-calling, mockery, and hostile humor.

» **Defensiveness** is a way of deflecting blame away from yourself and onto your partner (or someone else) by either counterattacking or whining and acting like an innocent victim.

» **Stonewalling** allows you to shut down and avoid responding altogether, or you respond in monosyllables or curt replies.

These behaviors can devolve into habitual responses during conflict or even show up in day-to-day conversation. They can be devastating and break down all intimacy and trust in the relationship.

Predictive Factor #3: Flooding

Flooding is a heightened state of arousal and agitation—a fight-or-flight response in reaction to the negative behaviors just outlined. These behaviors can feel so overwhelming and sudden that you become shell-shocked.

The breakdown of a relationship can be predicted by the combination of habitual harsh startups and frequent flooding, triggered by the regular presence of criticism, contempt, defensiveness, and stonewalling. Although each of these factors alone can predict a divorce, they usually coexist in an unhappy marriage or love relationship.

Predictive Factor #4: Body Reactions to Flooding

Dr. Gottman monitored couples during a conflict discussion to check for bodily changes and saw how physically distressing flooding was—making it impossible to work through conflict.

During a flooding episode, the heart speeds up to more than 100 beats per minute, even as high as 165. Blood pressure increases, and hormonal changes are triggered, including the secretion of adrenaline.

These physical sensations make it challenging to have a productive, cooperative discussion that leads to resolution.

Predictive Factor #5: Failed Repair Attempts

According to Dr. Gottman, divorce can often be predicted by listening to a single conversation between partners. By analyzing a couple's conflict, you can pick up on the pattern they tend to follow when communicating and working to resolve the conflict.

Part of this pattern includes the repair attempts the couple makes and whether these attempts succeed or fail. These are attempts the couple makes to reduce the tension and acrimony during a discussion. If these attempts fail, it is a fairly accurate predictor for an unhappy future.

Predictive Factor #6: Bad Memories about Your History

During Dr. Gottman's interviews with couples, he asks them to talk about the history of their relationship. Couples who tend to look back fondly on their early days also tend to have happier relationships.

They easily recall the positive feelings of love, excitement, and admiration they felt for each other. When discussing difficulties or challenges they've experienced, they view the struggles through a positive lens, drawing commitment and strength from the tough times they've gone through together.

Couples who can't recollect and share positive memories and who view past challenges with negativity tend to have less happy and successful marriages.

As you can see, many of the behaviors in Dr. Gottman's six predictors relate to unconscious, destructive habits fueled by strong emotions and low self-control. Unable to interact in a mindful and healthy way, couples lose motivation to spend time together, to be affectionate, and to acknowledge and praise one another.

They wind up having more negative interactions than positive, leaving both partners feeling disengaged and self-protective. The further the couple pulls apart, the more deeply entrenched they become in these negative relationship habits, as they have lost the buffers of trust and intimacy.

These negative habits must be unlearned and replaced with new, more positive habits to steer the relationship in a new direction. Sometimes this requires working with a counselor or other helping professional to address the underlying emotions, wounds, and misconceptions that trigger harmful behaviors.

But even without the help of a counselor, motivated couples can learn more mindful ways of interacting with each other that promote healing and connection rather than division. They can use these new habits to replace some of the destructive behaviors that creep into their interactions with each other.

One of the main reasons relationships fail is that couples don't intervene *soon enough* to address the problems and negative behaviors. They might sense that things aren't going well, but they aren't sure what to do about it, or they feel too uncomfortable to stir the pot further. They fail to take action to protect and heal the relationship at the first signs of distress, allowing negative patterns to take a foothold.

Our hope with this book is to help you to *become more aware* of unhealthy, unconscious patterns in your relationship, to *let go of old behaviors* that aren't serving you, and to *practice being more mindful about your relationship by engaging in positive new habits.*

Even if there are underlying issues that you and your partner need to work on, you can set the stage for healing and growth in your relationship by simply changing some of your behaviors and seeking to revive the good relationship habits you had early on.

A strong, happy, evolved relationship is definitely something worth fighting for and prioritizing in your life. In the next chapter, we'll share why improving your relationship will upgrade your entire life.

The Benefits of Building a Mindful Relationship

From personal experience, both Barrie and Steve know what it's like to be in a marriage lacking in mindfulness and how unconsciousness as a couple leads to disconnection and ultimately divorce. We understand how an unhappy love relationship can make the rest of your life feel pretty bleak.

Fortunately, we are each now in happy, healthy relationships and are highly motivated to use what we learned from our past marriages to ensure we are more present and proactive in our current relationships.

When you've experienced relationship failure, you feel compelled to "get it right" the next time, and you recognize how important it is to tend to the connection every day like it's a prized garden. Water it regularly, give it plenty of sun, pull the weeds quickly, and admire the beauty.

Avoiding the pain of a divorce or breakup is a good reason to be mindful in your relationship, but it shouldn't be the main impetus for your diligence. There are many more positive motivators for putting in this effort, not the least of which is your love for this person you are sharing your life with.

Here are some additional benefits of having a healthy, happy, and intentional marriage or committed relationship:

Benefit #1: Better Physical Health

Numerous studies confirm that happily married people enjoy better health than those who have never been married, particularly men. You don't have to be legally married. A long-term, committed relationship has the same positive effects on your physical health.

Marriage has been associated with a lower risk of disease, from diabetes to cardiovascular and respiratory problems. Married couples also tend to drink and smoke less and eat healthier foods. Being in a committed relationship also provides a buffer to the major stressors of life that typically impact physical health.

These benefits only apply to couples that are in happy marriages or relationships. Other research has shown that those who are in unhappy, stressful relationships have higher levels of inflammation, which is linked to a variety of ailments.

Benefit #2: A Longer Life

If you want to live longer, stay happily married or in a committed, long-term relationship. More research has shown that committed couples were 15–20% less likely to die prematurely than the population as a whole.

When you're in a relationship, your spouse or partner pays attention to your health and well-being, reminding you to see a doctor or cut back on the Oreos. Also, your partner's good habits influence you. If he or she stops smoking, you are more likely to quit too.

Again, studies show that living longer applies to happy couples—not conflict-ridden couples, twice as likely to die prematurely.

Benefit #3: Increased Wealth

If you want to improve your financial situation, stay in your marriage or committed relationship. Research shows that those who get married and stay married have nearly double the wealth of those who never marry. If you count combined household income, that adds up to four times the wealth.

On a personal note, Steve noticed that in 2012 when he first started dating his wife, his business income grew exponentially. He attributes that largely to becoming more grounded and giving up on many habits that he had while being single that were hurting his success (i.e., staying up late, eating junk food, drinking excessively).

When you are married or cohabiting, you share the expenses of one household rather than two individual households, cutting costs in half. If one partner needs to go back to school or stop working for some reason, there is someone there to pick up the slack.

However, if you get married and then divorce, you'll be in a worse financial situation than if you never married in the first place, according to the same research.

Benefit #4: Better Mental Health

Married people report less loneliness and depression. They are also less likely to abuse drugs and alcohol.

When you have a loving and supportive partner, you have someone with whom you can share life problems and challenges, reducing anxiety and stress.

You also have a larger support network when you're in a relationship, as each partner brings his or her own circle of family and friends into the relationship.

Benefit #5: Increased Happiness

Recent research has shown that marriage is positively correlated with personal well-being and happiness. The effects are particularly profound during middle age, when partners must cope with family demands and career stress.

The study indicates that "marriage may help ease the causes of the midlife dip in life satisfaction and that the benefits of marriage are unlikely to be short-lived."

Benefit #6: Satisfying Sex

Although it is true that the frequency of sex declines over time in long-term relationships, there is a greater potential for satisfying sex in happy, committed relationships.

Research has shown that couples can keep the passion alive and have a great sex life for the long term if they are proactive and make a conscious effort. The findings indicate that "foreplay, setting the mood, mixing it up, and expressing love are all factors that satisfied couples said they do regularly."

According to marital and sex therapists Michael Metz and Barry McCarthy in their book, *Enduring Desire*, couples who have been together for 15 years or longer enjoy the best sex. Over time you learn more about one another sexually, and you have fewer inhibitions to exploring and experimenting.

Unhappy, conflict-oriented couples are less likely to have satisfying sex or frequent sex. "There is a feedback relationship in most couples between happiness and having sex. Happy couples have more sex, and the more sex a couple has, the happier they report being," explains Denise A. Donnelly, associate professor of sociology at Georgia State University in an article for *The New York Times*.

Benefit #7: Happier, More Successful Kids

If you and your partner regularly engage in destructive conflict that includes verbal aggression like yelling, name calling, insults, and threats of abandonment, your children are more likely to have mental, emotional, and social problems growing up, according to research.

Even passive forms of conflict, like avoidance, walking out, sulking, withdrawing, or capitulation can have a long-term negative impact on kids. These passive-aggressive behaviors can be even more stressful and disturbing to children who know something is wrong but don't understand what it is or why it's happening.

However, occasional conflict in front of children that involves support, compromise, and positive communication can help them develop better social skills and improve self-esteem and emotional security. These positive behaviors lead to better performance in school and later success in life.

It's clear that if you want to be healthier, wealthier, and happier and want to live longer and have successful, happy kids, it's worth the investment of your time and energy to develop better relationship habits and unlearn the habits that are detrimental to your relationship. So if you want to learn how to build these habits, read the next chapter and then dive into the 25 mindful habits that you can build into your relationship.

How to Build Mindful
Relationship Habits

We both talk frequently about how to build habits in our previous books. But if you haven't read any of our other titles, then we recommend using this eight-step plan to make sure you stick with any new routine you're trying to incorporate into your busy day.

Step 1: Focus Only on Relationship Habits

There is a concept called ego depletion, which is "a person's diminished capacity to regulate their thoughts, feelings and actions."

Ego depletion impacts our ability to form new habits because our supply of willpower is spread out among all the areas of our lives. To counter this, it's important to work on only one habit at a time. That way, your store of willpower can be channeled into building that one habit, increasing your odds of success.

To keep things simple, we ask that you completely focus on forming just relationship habits, which means you should avoid adding anything "new" to your schedule. That way, these mindful practices will have 100% of your attention.

Step #2: Commit to One Habit for 30 Days

Some people say it takes 21 days to build a habit, while others claim it takes up to 66 days. The truth is that the length of time really varies from person to person and habit to habit. You'll find that some habits are easy to build, while others require more effort. Our advice is to commit to mindfulness for the next 30 days (or a month, to keep it simple).

Step #3: Anchor Your Mindful Practices to Established Habits

Your relationship efforts should **not** be based upon motivation, fads, or temporary desire. Instead, these behaviors should be instilled in your life where it becomes automatic behavior.

The simplest way to do this is to incorporate the teachings of BJ Fogg and his "Tiny Habits" concept. What you want to do is to commit to a very small habit change and take baby steps as you build on it. An important aspect of his teaching is to "anchor" the new habit to something you *already* do on a daily basis.

For example: *"When I get home from work, my wife and I will enjoy a quiet meal, free from distractions, where we share what happened during the day."*

You get the idea. Simply find a habit you already do consistently, and then anchor your new behavior to it.

Step #4: Pick a Time for Your Relationship Habit

The best time for working on your relationship is the time that works best for the both of you. That said, keep in mind that any new habit should occur immediately after your trigger so you'll be reminded to follow through on a daily basis.

Be sure your trigger is something that happens every day. If you want to skip weekends or take a day off, you can certainly do that, but it will take longer for the habit to form.

So if you decide to work on your relationship after dinner, the trigger could be when you clean up after the meal or at a set time each evening (e.g., 8 p.m.).

Step #5: Take Baby Steps

As discussed in Tiny Habits, the best way to create a new routine is to make micro-commitments and focus on small wins. Motivation alone won't help. The danger of relying on motivation alone is that you don't have a backup plan for when you're not in the mood (or you're too tired) to work on your relationship. Instead, you need to turn the habit into an automatic behavior.

So while your long-term goal is to improve many aspects of your relationship, you should start slow and focus on building the routine first. It's more important to stay consistent and not miss a day than it is to have an hour-long conversation one day and ignore each other the rest of the week.

What we recommend is to focus on small wins that will help build the practice of being open with one another and sharing your thoughts.

Examples include:

» giving a foot rub to your partner every night while watching television

» turning off your cell phones during dinnertime

» preparing your partner's favorite tea or coffee in the morning

» texting a thoughtful comment daily

Yes, these activities seem overly simplistic. That's the idea here! You want to commit to something so easy that it's *impossible* to miss a day. Then, when you've built the habit, you can focus on building one of the 25 relationship habits that we recommend in this book.

Step #6: Plan for Your Obstacles

Every new routine will have obstacles. When you know in advance what your obstacles are, you can take preventive action to overcome them. Examples of the common issues that couples encounter include:

» feeling too tired (or "not in the mood") to talk

» turning a conversation into an argument

» not having enough time to dedicate to your relationship

» experiencing anger or resentment toward your partner

If you anticipate these obstacles, you won't be blindsided by them.

The simplest solution is to use a concept called "If-Then Planning" where you create scripts to help you overcome these obstacles. Here are some examples:

» "If I frequently feel tired before a scheduled conversation, we will schedule a new time when we'll both feel awake and refreshed."

» "If we rarely have time to talk, we will both eliminate the least important activity from our schedules."

» "If either of us starts to feel anger or resentment, we will take a five-minute break to cool off."

See how each of these statements helps you overcome the specific challenges that you face? Our advice is to create similar statements for all the roadblocks that might arise with your daily relationship habit.

Step #7: Create Accountability for Your Relationship Habits

According to the Hawthorne Effect, you're more likely to follow through with a commitment when others are observing you. That said, this can be hard to do if you don't want the whole world to know you're working on your relationship.

So one suggestion is to create an anonymous account on apps like Chains and Coach.me to track your progress, work with an accountability partner, or post regular updates to an online community related to the habit. Do whatever it takes to get reinforcement from others in support of your new routine.

Never underestimate the power of social approval. Simply *knowing* you will be held accountable for your habit keeps you focused and consistent.

Step #8: Reward Important Milestones

Building mindfulness into your relationship doesn't have to be boring. Instead, you can make it fun and enjoyable by building a reward system where you both celebrate those important milestones in your relationship.

The reward you pick is up to you, but it's important to celebrate those big moments along the way. Keep in mind that a reward doesn't have to break the bank. You could check out a new movie, enjoy a night out with your significant other, or simply do something you love that doesn't cost a lot of money.

If you get stuck, Steve has a list of 155 ways to reward yourself on his blog.

We tend to underestimate the importance of having "fun" while building habits. Often, though, having a clear reward for regularly completing an action will help you to stick to the new routine.

Those are the eight steps for forming positive relationship habits. Simply follow the steps outlined and determine the best time to perform your habit, and you'll quickly add this routine to your day.

Now that you understand the basics of habit formation, let's dive into specific mindful habits that you can build into your relationship.

Mindful Relationship Habit #1
Prioritize Your Relationship with Meetings

We discussed previously how essential it is to prioritize your marriage or intimate relationship above everything else in your life. It is central to your own health, happiness, and success, as well as to those close to you.

Most of us would say we put our relationship first, but do we actually do that?

Do we regularly prioritize our relationship and our spouse or partner ahead of work, digital devices, personal interests, and other people?

Are we willing to sacrifice our time, energy, and emotional comfort to make sure we don't compromise the intimacy, trust, respect, and love we share with our partner?

Prioritizing your relationship takes commitment and effort. It is a multifaceted habit that involves many (or most) of the other practices we outline in this book. You may say you prioritize your relationship, but if you aren't taking daily action to *show* you are serious, then your words don't mean much.

However, we have found one habit that is central to prioritizing your relationship and ensuring you keep the health of your connection on the front burner.

That habit is having regular meetings with your partner to assess how things are going between you—what's working well, what needs to change, and what you need to work on to heal any rifts or hurt feelings.

This is not a meeting to discuss your kids, your to-do lists, or your upcoming vacation. It's a meeting solely to work on your relationship and identify ways you can make it stronger and better, and it should be the very first habit you establish together.

Your relationship meeting will be the perfect time to discuss the habit work you are doing with this book and how you are progressing with your goals as a couple.

How to Develop This Habit

If you are going through a difficult challenge or conflict, you should meet every day until you feel like things are back on track and you've reached a resolution. Otherwise, consider meeting weekly or twice monthly. Set aside an hour for the meeting, even if you don't end up using the entire hour.

Discuss a day and a time of day that work well for both of you.

Choose a time when you are less likely to be interrupted by children, work, or other life demands. Also, think about a time when you aren't stressed or under pressure. In the morning before you leave for work would likely *not* be a good time. A Sunday morning or an evening after kids are in bed might be better.

Set up a reminder system or trigger for the meeting.

This is especially important if you are just meeting weekly or twice monthly. It's easy to forget a habit that you don't do every day if it's not on your calendar with a clear reminder.

Make sure both of you put this meeting on your schedules for the entire year, and try not to allow anything (except emergencies) to get in the way of this meeting. If you are traveling, or if you absolutely have to miss a meeting for an important reason, reschedule it as soon as possible, even if it's on another day.

The one tool that Steve recommends is Google Calendar. He and his wife use this tool to share their schedule, including meetings, appointments, and upcoming events related to their son. This makes it pretty handy for both of them to know exactly what the other person is doing at any point in the day.

Start small, and make it simple.

When you first start having these regular meetings, choose a relationship habit you both want to work on that is easy and small, like hugging for two minutes every day or complimenting each other at night before bed.

For the first week, just work on your one habit to get the hang of it. Your next meeting to discuss your progress may not take very long, but you will enjoy the early success of your efforts.

Take notes in a journal during the meeting.

Both of you should take notes during the meetings to keep track of your progress. This allows you to see how your connection and intimacy are improving and to note what you need to continue working on.

It also helps you remember what you both agree to work on during the days or weeks between meetings. Jot down brief notes during the meeting, and then go back and expand your notes afterward if necessary.

During the time in between meetings, you can write down observations, concerns, or situations you want to discuss in the next meeting.

Set the tone for the meeting.

The last thing you want this meeting to become is a forum for arguing and defensiveness. The goal is to create a positive, respectful atmosphere where you can talk openly (but kindly) without fear of being attack or diminished.

Begin the meeting with a hug and words of love and affirmation. Try not to bring any strong feelings of anger into the meeting—although one or both of you may have irritations or frustrations to discuss.

Try to avoid engaging in arguments or difficult discussions before the meeting so you don't bring in any added negative energy. If you feel too angry to have a positive interaction, then delay the meeting until you feel calmer.

Choose a space for the meeting that is conducive to private, productive, respectful conversation where both partners feel on equal footing.

Remove all distractions, like your computers and phones. Make sure anyone else in the house knows not to interrupt you.

Begin with the positives.

We suggest starting the discussion on a positive note by reviewing everything that went well for your relationship the preceding day or week. Share specific things your partner did or said that you liked, how these words or behaviors made you feel, and how you felt they enhanced your relationship.

For example, you might compliment your partner on consistently giving you a hug and kiss before leaving for work each morning. This gesture made you feel cherished and loved, and it improved your relationship by starting the day out on a close and tender note.

Both of you should prepare prior to the meeting to share one or more of these positive situations or encounters. They might relate to something specific you agreed to work on from a previous meeting (like one of the other habits outlined in this book), or simply a behavior you noticed and liked.

Have an agenda for the meeting.

Your meetings will be far more productive if you know what you want to accomplish—whether individually or mutually or both.

If you are working on establishing a new habit to improve your relationship, discuss this habit next, after you talk about the positives. Take turns sharing how well you think you did with this new behavior and how well you think your partner did.

If there is an area where you felt your partner didn't follow through as promised or expected, this is the time to bring it up and ask for a change. Try to frame these complaints and requests in a positive way rather than as a criticism or demand. Reinforce positive behavior and ask for more of it.

For example, you might say, "I really appreciate that you were so affectionate on Wednesday when we were watching TV together. I need more affection like that and would love for you to cuddle with me when we are in bed before we fall asleep. Are you willing to do that?"

If you are receiving a request from your partner that is reasonable, try your best to honor the request and work on the behavior. Don't allow selfishness, defensiveness, or stubbornness to prevent you from showing your love to your partner in this way.

If you can't honor the request the way it's presented, offer what you are willing to do and seek a compromise. Both of you should make notes about what you are agreeing to work on in the coming days or weeks. You will read more about communicating requests and making compromises later in the book.

You also may have a problem or issue you want to discuss that doesn't relate to a habit you're working on. For example, your partner may have said something hurtful or might have neglected you in some way. Bring this up by using the "I feel" statements we cover in Habit #17. You might say, "When you teased me in front of your parents on Saturday, I felt embarrassed and put down. Will you please not do that again?"

It's very important that neither of you try to minimize your partner's feelings by defending or deflecting your behavior or by denying that your partner's feelings are justified. Your teasing comment may have been innocent, but your partner's feelings should be your priority.

Note: Try not to cover more than one or two big issues or behavior change requests during each meeting so neither of you feels overwhelmed. You both want to be successful in your efforts, and you will be more successful by addressing a few changes at a time.

Review your work for the coming week.

Depending on what you covered in the meeting and the work you both need to do, outline the actions you need to take during the week to make improvements. Write these down in your journals for review the following week. Then end the meeting the same way you began it—with a hug, a kiss, and words of affirmation.

These meetings are an essential part of your progress in strengthening your connection and enhancing your communication and understanding of one another.

If you are working through this book without your partner, have the meeting by yourself to see how you are doing in establishing habits that YOU want to develop within the relationship. Show your journal and the work you are doing to your partner, and perhaps he or she will be inspired to join in.

Mindful Relationship Habit #2
Learn Emotional Intelligence

You've probably heard the term "emotional intelligence" used in relation to career performance, leadership, and success. But your level of emotional intelligence (EQ) has a profound impact on your relationship satisfaction and success, according to a number of studies. It is essential for cultivating a conscious, evolved connection with your partner.

In his book, *Emotional Intelligence: Why It Can Matter More Than IQ*, psychologist Daniel Goleman suggests that EQ may be more important than IQ, since standard intelligence scores are quite narrow and don't reflect the full scope of human intelligence.

Our ability to relate well with other people, particularly our intimate partners, has more to do with our long-term success and happiness than our reasoning and analytical abilities.

Goleman's book popularized the importance of EQ, but the term "emotional intelligence" was originally created by two psychologists and researchers, Peter Salovey and John Mayer, who pioneered this new view of what intelligence encompasses.

Emotional intelligence includes the ability to express and control our emotions, as well as the ability to understand, interpret, and respond to the emotions of others. Salovey and Mayer devised a model with four factors that they believe comprise emotional intelligence.

1. **Perceiving Emotions:** To understand emotions, you need to perceive them accurately. This perception can involve understanding nonverbal cues, like body language and facial expressions.

2. **Reasoning with Emotions:** This step involves using your emotions to prompt thinking, reasoning, and analysis. Emotions help us prioritize what we pay attention to and react to and how we respond emotionally to these things.

3. **Understanding Emotions:** The emotions we perceive from others can reflect many things. If someone is showing anger, we have to interpret the cause of their anger and what it might mean. This involves a more sophisticated ability to discern various possible reasons without jumping to conclusions.

4. **Managing Emotions:** Your ability to manage emotions effectively is a crucial part of EQ, especially when it comes to your love relationship. Regulating your own emotions and responding appropriately to the emotions of others are part of emotional management.

So what does all of this mean for you and your partner?

When you both work to develop the skills of emotional intelligence and apply them to your relationship, you increase self-awareness, learn to manage your emotions in heated or difficult situations, and develop abilities such as empathy and active listening that make you more caring and effective partners.

Developing your EQ is a lifelong process that involves creating many new habits, not just one. Unlike IQ, which doesn't change significantly over a lifetime, your EQ can evolve and increase as you continue to learn and grow within your relationship.

The longer you work on developing these EQ habits over time, the more intimate and satisfying your relationship will become. It should be no surprise that low EQ in one or both partners is correlated with relationship dissatisfaction.

Below is a list of emotional intelligence habits that you might want to focus on. Take a moment to read through the list, and make notes about where you might need some work.

» Managing and regulating your emotions, especially during stress or conflict

» Speaking kindly and respectfully to your partner

» Reading nonverbal cues like facial expressions and body language

» Expressing your own emotions calmly and clearly

» Expressing physical affection

» Having a realistic sense of your own strengths and weaknesses

» Having relationship goals and values

» Having self-assurance and confidence

» Being able to laugh at yourself

» Showing empathy and sympathy for your partner

» Listening attentively and actively to your partner without becoming defensive

» Showing a consistent willingness to follow through on commitments

» Practicing flexibility and compromise

» Initiating conflict resolution

» Showing interest in your partner and his or her interests

» Sharing equally in household tasks and responsibilities

» Being trustworthy

» Being vulnerable with your partner

» Apologizing and forgiving easily

We cover many of these EQ habits in more detail later, so if you decide to work on one of these, be sure to read the related information in this book. Let's go over how you can work on developing the habits of emotional intelligence to improve your relationship.

How to Develop This Habit

Start by choosing the EQ habit you want to work on.

Look through the list of behaviors and decide where you need the most improvement in your emotional intelligence.

» Do you have trouble controlling your emotions?

» Is it difficult to express how you feel?

» Do you get easily defensive or critical?

» Do you frequently neglect to honor your word?

Choose just one behavior to focus on at a time, as it will feel overwhelming trying to change too many new habits at once. Speak with your partner and ask him or her where you need to focus your efforts, as you may have a blind spot to your own EQ weaknesses.

You may not agree with your partner's assessment, but if your partner sees a lack of skill in this area, then working on it can only improve your relationship and your partner's trust in you.

Write down your past low EQ behaviors.

Make a list of all your past behaviors that show a lack of emotional intelligence related to the skill you want to work on. For example, if you want to express your emotions more clearly and calmly, how have you been expressing them in ways that aren't clear and calm? What are some specific examples?

Again, you may want to ask your partner for feedback, as he or she may have more awareness around the specific behaviors than you do. It may be hard to hear this feedback, but it's important to look honestly at your own behaviors before you can change them.

Just being mindful about how you are behaving with low emotional intelligence can go a long way in motivating you to change bad habits into better ones.

Commit to a new EQ habit you want to develop.

Isolating a specific new habit and working on it regularly can be difficult because so many relationship habits occur in response to unplanned situations or conversations that trigger you.

However, if you make a point of proactively practicing a new habit every day, even when you aren't triggered by circumstances, you will find it becomes a more natural response when situations arise organically.

For example, going back to the habit of expressing your emotions more clearly and calmly, it may be hard to remember to perform this new habit every time the situation merits it. But if you decide in advance that you will express yourself this way at a particular time every day, then you will train yourself to make this new behavior more automatic when you need to use it.

It may feel awkward and out of context to approach your spouse at 4:00 each day and say something like, "I feel frustrated when you spend so much time on your computer and neglect to connect with me." But if you tell your spouse you are working on this habit, he or she will be more receptive to your efforts.

Some EQ skills will be easier than others to practice on a daily schedule, such as showing physical affection or speaking kindly to your spouse. The point is, regardless of the skill you are working on, you want to do something every day to reinforce the new behavior, even if it feels a bit stilted at first.

Use the rubber band method for changing your behavior.

Review the list of your past low EQ behaviors related to the habit you want to develop. If you have been practicing these behaviors for a long time, they have likely become a knee-jerk, unconscious response to your partner.

It will take some effort to unlearn these bad habits, so we suggest the "rubber band" technique to help you. Put a rubber band on your wrist, and every time you notice yourself reverting to low EQ behaviors related to your new habit, move the rubber band from one wrist to the other or gently pop it on your wrist. This physical interruption of the behavior reminds you to stop what you are doing and replace the old habit with the new one.

For example, if you want to start speaking in a kinder manner, and you notice yourself saying something unkind, stop yourself and move the rubber band. Apologize to your partner, and tell him or her you want to begin again. Then rephrase what you want to say in a kinder way.

Ask your partner for accountability.

Communicating with your partner will help you stay committed to your efforts, especially if he or she encourages this positive habit. Tell your partner exactly what you are working on and how you plan to build this new behavior.

During your regular relationship meetings, ask your partner for feedback on how you are doing with your new habit and how your efforts have made him or her feel. You can make alterations to your habit work based on the feedback you are getting, if necessary.

Move on to another EQ habit after a few weeks.

Once this first new EQ habit has become more automatic and natural for you, then you can begin working on another EQ behavior. Go through the same steps outlined here, and continue to practice the first habit in more organic situations that previously triggered a low EQ response from you.

> **Note:** To learn more about emotional intelligence in relationships, we suggest that you read Dr. Goleman's book *Social Intelligence: The New Science of Human Relationships* to get a better understanding of how your EQ impacts your relationships.

Mindful Relationship Habit #3
Create a Relationship Vision

Do you and your partner have goals and dreams about your relationship and your lives together as a couple? Do you know how you want to improve your connection and make it stronger?

Crafting a relationship vision forces you to be more mindful because it requires you to define your goals and expectations and creates purpose and direction in your relationship. It allows you to be intentional and proactive about every part of your lives together.

By first creating individual relationship visions and discussing them together, you can craft a *mutual vision* that prioritizes shared goals and dreams, as well as makes room for each partner's individual needs.

A vision allows you to establish ground rules, boundaries, priorities, and plans for honoring your needs on a daily basis. It helps you bypass some of the arguments that arise from misunderstandings and divergent expectations by addressing them before they come up during conflict.

Creating a mutual vision is also a great training exercise for boosting your emotional intelligence as you learn to negotiate, compromise, clarify, and communicate as a team with a shared intention.

More important, your vision will serve as a "relationship roadmap," revealing whether or not you are on track with your goals and when you might need to take corrective measures to realign your lives with your vision.

We all have some preconceptions about what our committed love relationship should be like. We've adopted ideas into our unconscious by observing our parents, our extended family, our neighbors, our friends, and even television and movies.

Prior to being married or in a committed relationship, your vision may have been simply to "live happily ever after." But by now, you probably realize things aren't that simple. Happily ever after takes some planning, compromise, and effort.

Creating your vision and working together to ensure that you live by it can reinforce your intimacy by giving you a shared purpose with shared goals.

It can become an impetus for regular meaningful conversations as you strive daily to align your words and actions with your vision. It can also help you navigate conflict and reach resolution more quickly because you have this blueprint to guide you.

How to Develop This Habit

At first, you and your partner will work on your visions separately. Once you complete your individual visions, you will come together to craft a shared vision for your relationship.

Choose a time that works for both of you to work on your visions for at least fifteen minutes a day until you complete them. You might want to work on one area (listed below) each day. Once you finish, you will come together to work on your shared vision during this same timeframe.

Keep these rules in mind as you write your vision.

It should be written:

- » in the present tense
- » in positive terms (what you want, not what you don't want)
- » in specific terms
- » using "we" statements

Examples might be:

- » "We go on a date night every week without the children and enjoy a romantic dinner."
- » "We will save $1,000 a month to put toward a down payment on a house in three years."
- » "We will take a weekend trip for just the two of us at least twice a year."

Have a clear sense of your values.

Before you begin working on your vision, define your top 5–10 core values for your relationship. These are the guiding principles that help you stay true to yourself and what you want for your marriage or relationship.

You can use this list of value words on Barrie's blog, Live Bold and Bloom, to help you define your own core values. Make a note of these core values, and as you write your vision, refer to them frequently to ensure your vision doesn't stray from these guiding principles.

Craft your vision for several areas of your relationship.

Using your values as a guide, consider your *ideal* goals and dreams for your marriage or relationship. Remember, this first effort is YOUR vision, so as you complete it, don't hold back on your own goals because you're not sure about your partner's vision. You will come back to creating a shared vision later on.

You can use bulleted phrases or thoughts, or write out complete sentences that tell the story of your vision for each of the areas below. As an example, under "emotional intimacy," a vision might be …

> *We can talk to each other about anything without fear of being shamed or judged. We are completely open and accepting of one another. My partner is my best friend, who understands me better than anyone, and I am the same for him. We feel safe and trusting with each other and are free to be ourselves. We enjoy meaningful talks together, sharing the ups and downs of life and working together toward common goals. We are a connected team but respect one another as individuals.*

Include the following aspects in your vision:

- » emotional intimacy
- » sexual intimacy
- » physical affection
- » romantic gestures
- » daily communication

» conflict discussion and resolution

» money, finances, spending, budgeting

» careers

» family time

» parenting

» extended family and friends

» mutual interests

» individual interests

» personal and relationship growth

» religion and spirituality

» goals, bucket list

» other

Work together on your shared relationship vision.

Once you complete your individual visions, use this habit time to create a shared vision. First, review your core values together. Make sure you are on the same page with most of them.

Then discuss your individual visions for each area, working on one area at a time. Write down any goals and dreams that you *both* included in your personal visions.

Finally, go back and discuss any goals that you have on your personal vision that your partner hasn't included. You may find you easily agree to include the goal in your shared vision. Or your partner may not share this goal, and this may require some discussion and negotiation.

You may want to save this negotiation for later in a weekly meeting and use this vision work time to get your mutual goals hammered out in the areas where you do agree.

Determine action steps to make your vision real.

Once you have completed your mutual vision, go back through each area to discuss the work you need to do as individuals and as a couple to make your vision real.

These action steps may be new habits that you will want to work on right away, or they may be goals for the future, like building a new house or taking more trips together. Write down your action steps for each area.

Some of your action steps may be covered in the habits outlined in this book, so be sure to review all the habits here to get ideas and strategies for developing the habits in your vision.

Prioritize your action steps.

Have a discussion about the vision goals and action steps you want to begin working on right away. Start by individually writing down your top five priorities. Then see if you and your partner share any priorities on your lists.

Hopefully, there will be at least one shared priority, and if so, this is the best place to begin your efforts. If not, you may need to draw straws or negotiate where you will start.

If your goal requires developing a new habit or changing behaviors, use our habit instructions earlier in the book to help you create a plan for success.

Some of your vision goals may be actions that happen infrequently or sporadically, like deciding to have monthly dinners with friends or having quarterly budget meetings. Because they are so infrequent, they don't require developing a habit. Just be sure to put them on your calendars so you don't forget.

Mindful Relationship Habit #4
Lead with Respect and Kindness

When Barrie's children were teenagers and would say something unkind or disrespectful to her, she would remind them that they would never speak to another adult this way. Wasn't their mother deserving of as much or more respect as any other adult?

Their counter argument was that they felt safe in expressing their anger or frustration this way because they knew, "Mom will always love me."

It's true that a parent's love is steadfast, even when children are acting out or being unpleasant. But as children grow up and mature, they learn how to control their emotions and words and can interact with their parents as adults.

In many ways, we revert to our teen years with our spouse or intimate partner. We feel safe letting off steam or saying something unkind because we assume this person will always be there and love us.

But Barrie's question to her children applies even more profoundly in a love relationship:

Isn't our partner deserving of as much or more respect as any other adult?

So ask yourself: are there unkind or disrespectful behaviors and words you use with your partner that you would never, ever use with another adult?

The answer is "yes" for most of us. We are willing to cross the line with our partners because we are so intimately involved with them and feel free to take out our frustrations and irritations on them without fear of serious consequences.

But if we do this too often, there are consequences. They might not be as immediate and direct as they were when you were disciplining your disrespectful teenager, but every act of disrespect and hurtful behavior takes a toll on your love relationship.

According to Dr. John Gottman's research, for every negative interaction between couples, it takes five positive ones to counteract the impact of the negative one. In other words, when you say or do something hurtful to your partner, the harm of this event isn't negated until the two of you have five loving and kind interactions.

Not many couples take the initiative to instigate five positive interactions every time there's a negative one, even if they know about this research. They accumulate layers of negative feelings and resentments that never get resolved or erased. This backlog of bad feelings erodes trust and intimacy, which will eventually doom the relationship.

Rather than having to counteract every negative behavior with five positive behaviors, wouldn't it make more sense to adopt a new mind-set about how you treat one another?

What if you treated your partner with the same kindness and respect in everyday life that you use with your boss, your best friend, or even your mom? What if you made the decision to be respectful, kind, and affirming, even during conflict or difficult conversations? Then you wouldn't have to try so hard to make up for the painful, divisive interactions that weaken the closeness you share together.

Of course, there will still be times when you feel angry or frustrated, but if you make the commitment to always lead with respect and kindness, you'll be less likely to fall into the bad habits that sabotage your connection.

You control your words and behaviors with your boss and friends, even when they irritate you. If you are motivated, you *can* learn this same self-control with your partner, the person you love the most and who is most deserving of your best behavior.

Practicing respect and kindness isn't just a nice thing to do. It makes a huge difference in the quality of your relationship. It builds mutual trust and fosters healthy communication. It allows you to manage conflict and challenges more effectively. Most importantly, it shows the depth of your love for your partner and the commitment you have to your relationship.

How to Develop This Habit

Do you and your partner agree that showing kindness and respect are essential for the health and happiness of your relationship? Are you both willing to practice the self-control needed to reduce the number of negative interactions between you and to prioritize kindness and mutual respect?

If so, it can be helpful to mentally revisit your courtship days when you were on your best behavior. Think about how loving, attentive, forgiving, considerate, deferential, and kind you were to one another. Try to put yourselves back in that mind-set, even if you have to "act" more kindly than you feel right now.

With practice, this new mind-set will have so many positive effects on your relationship that it will become natural and desirable for both of you. For now, you just need to believe that it's a worthy endeavor.

Choose your habit.

There are hundreds of ways to show kindness and respect to your partner. Speaking loving and affirming words, showing common courtesies, listening attentively, offering praise and gratitude, and being quick to apologize are just a few. So how do you know where to begin developing this new habit?

Perhaps the best place to begin is where you and your partner feel the *least* respected by the other. Maybe one of you feels the other is too harsh or critical. Or you might feel your partner doesn't pay enough attention when you talk.

Both of you can write down one way (just one for now) you feel disrespected by your partner by completing the sentence: "I feel disrespected when my partner …"

Then complete the sentence: "I would like my partner to show me more respect in this area by …" Fill in the behavior or words you would like to see more of from your partner.

For example, you might say:

"I feel disrespected when my partner doesn't acknowledge me when I walk into the room."

Or "I would like my partner to show me more respect in this area by looking up, smiling, and saying something positive to me when I come into the room."

Show your requests to one another to determine if you are both willing to work on the new habit your partner has requested. If not, suggest what you are willing to do to work on developing the habit.

Decide how you will implement this habit.

If your partner has requested that you do something daily, like having a five-minute conversation before you both leave for work or helping more with the dinner cleanup in the evening, then you can work on this new behavior as you would any other habit.

Choose a time of day to perform the habit, a trigger for performing it, and some form of accountability. For example, a trigger for a five-minute conversation before work could be pouring your first cup of coffee in the morning, and accountability could happen during your weekly meetings with your partner.

However, your partner's request might involve a behavior that is more sporadic, such as putting your phone down and making eye contact when he or she is talking to you. Because this situation occurs at different times and requires dropping a bad habit and replacing it, you may need a cue or reminder from your partner to help you stay on track.

You don't want to be dependent on this reminder forever, since the goal is to adopt a new way of behaving permanently. But initially, you may need some help. So talk together about what your partner should say or do if you neglect to perform the new habit. This could be a verbal reminder, a single word, or even a hand signal.

Once you're aware that you've neglected the habit, go back and repeat the situation again using the desired habit behavior. If your partner walks into the room and you forget to put down your phone and use eye contact, then your partner should walk out and come in again so you can practice the habit and reinforce it.

Discuss your habit work.

At your weekly meetings, talk together about how your efforts with kindness and respect habits are impacting your feelings for each other and the quality of your relationship.

Also discuss the habit and how you are doing with your efforts. Are you remembering to follow through? Does anything need to shift or change to make the habit work easier or more effective? Is the habit beginning to feel more automatic?

Move on to another kindness and respect habit.

Once you find that your initial habit feels more natural to perform, you can begin working on another habit to show more kindness and respect to one another.

You may find that working on the initial habit has motivated you to be kinder and more respectful of one another in general. A little civility and consideration can go a long way and inspire you to step up your game in many other ways.

A more difficult habit to develop is practicing respect and kindness during conflict or times when you feel irritable, stressed, or ill. Discuss how you might be treating one another disrespectfully during these times, and determine new behaviors you want to practice when these situations arise.

It will be harder to follow through when you are emotionally triggered or feeling bad, but you can still harness enough self-control to excuse yourself in order to calm down or to take a deep breath rather than lashing out. We'll discuss this in greater detail in Habit #20 on managing anger.

Mindful Relationship Habit #5
Practice Acceptance of Your Partner

Think back to those magical days when you and your partner first fell in love and you thought he or she was practically perfect in every way. This person was the complete package—exactly what you were hoping for. You didn't notice any flaws, or if you did, you were quick to overlook or diminish them.

Over time, however, you were shocked to learn that your partner was indeed flawed. You wondered, "When did he change? What happened to her?" But the truth is, your partner didn't change. You did. As the haze of infatuation evaporated, you were faced with a cold, stark reality—your perfect lover is human after all.

And even more shocking—your partner has had the same disappointing revelation about you. He or she no longer views you as perfect and unblemished. Your flaws and frailties are now painfully exposed.

What you once viewed as endearing or fascinating in your partner is now irritating or boring. The little quirks that were so cute and unique suddenly drive you crazy. However, it's the *perception* you have of your partner that has shifted over time. Your partner has had these behaviors and quirks all along, and yet you were able to see past them in the beginning. So why can't you now?

It's at this point in a romance that many couples start to bicker and try to change one another, building resentments and frustration about perceived imperfections. You long to stuff your partner back into the ideal image you had of him or her, unaware that the ideal was an illusion all along.

It's painful to realize your perfect partner is an imperfect human being. But once that reality becomes clear, you have two choices. You can make each other miserable by criticizing, blaming, and coercing change, or you can use this awareness as the catalyst for a new and more evolved kind of relationship.

From our earliest years, we all seek approval and acceptance—first from our parents, then our peers, and later on from our love partners. Once we concede that our spouse or partner is not merely an extension of ourselves and our egos, but rather a unique and worthy individual who deserves our acceptance, then we can enjoy a deeper and more intimate connection.

When we fully embrace this beautifully flawed individual, and he or she accepts us, the relationship becomes much more effortless and enjoyable.

You don't feel threatened by your differing opinions or interests. Your ego isn't bruised when your partner doesn't behave exactly as you would. In fact, you come to love and appreciate the unique differences in one another. You love your partner for the person he or she is—not who you want them to be.

Both partners must be willing to practice acceptance of the other to establish an intimate and joyful connection. If you have ever experienced dissatisfaction or shaming from your partner (or anyone), you know how painful this rejection feels. No one wants to feel they are unacceptable as they are or be coerced to change.

Practicing acceptance doesn't mean you can't hope for positive change in certain areas or even ask for it respectfully. But whether or not the change is forthcoming, you must respect your partner as an individual with free will. There are some areas where you and your partner can be flexible, and others where you can't, but you both deserve love and acceptance regardless.

How to Develop This Habit

Learning to accept your partner is an essential way of showing your esteem and love. It is a way of honoring this unique individual rather than demanding he or she become a clone of you. It takes some effort and self-restraint to practice acceptance, but once you master the skill, you will see how positively it impacts your partner and your relationship.

Adopting this habit requires practicing a new mind-set in which you consciously turn your attention away from your assumptions, disappointments, and frustrations with your partner and toward your love and admiration for him or her.

Here are some strategies for reinforcing this new mind-set.

List your partner's positive qualities.

Sit down with a journal or notebook and list all of the positive qualities and attributes you appreciate and love about each other. Write down anything and everything you can think of, getting as specific as possible.

Some ideas to help you get started include:

- » loving and kind behaviors
- » romantic gestures
- » good character traits
- » sense of humor
- » intelligence and creativity
- » interests and skills
- » good parenting skills
- » appearance and style
- » empathy and compassion
- » patience
- » work ethic
- » shared values
- » career successes and abilities
- » sexual desirability
- » authenticity and openness
- » reliability
- » loyalty in friendships
- » love of extended family members
- » ability to forgive and forget
- » showing interest in you and your interests
- » a positive attitude and thirst for life
- » a sense of give and take
- » a great laugh or smile
- » self-discipline and tenacity

Once you have your list completed, take a few minutes to reflect on each of these positive qualities, how much you appreciate them, and how they enhance your life and relationship.

Review your list with your partner.

After you have finished your lists, find a time when you won't be interrupted or distracted and read your lists to one another. If you can think of specific examples to share with your partner, talk about these and how much you like or appreciate them. Ask your partner to talk about how it makes him or her feel to hear the things on your list. Notice how your praise and focus on these positive qualities impacts your partner's attitude, as well as your own.

Keep this list in a place you can refer to it quickly when you find yourself frustrated with or disappointed in your partner.

Work on your negative thinking habits.

If you have gotten in the habit of thinking negative thoughts about your partner and feeling (or acting) critical, disappointed, irritated, or judgmental, then you need to work on changing your thought patterns and the words and behaviors they foster.

The rubber band method mentioned in Habit #2 will help you change these negative thinking habits. Put a rubber band on your wrist as a reminder to pay attention to your thoughts about your spouse or partner.

When you catch yourself mentally grumbling about him or her, move the rubber band to your other wrist or gently pop it to interrupt your thoughts. Then grab your list of qualities you love about your partner and reflect on them rather than focusing on the negative.

In time, you won't need the rubber band or the list. You will automatically realize when you are indulging in negative thoughts about your partner and will quickly remind yourself of all of his or her good qualities.

Address black-and-white assumptions.

One of the most common causes for conflict in relationships is when one partner believes he or she knows the "right" way to do things, while the other partner is doing it all "wrong."

You may assume you know best, have the correct solution, or know what is right for your partner. This black-and-white thinking reveals a lack of respect for your partner and an unwillingness to accept him or her as a unique and capable individual.

Adopting this habit involves a willingness to let go of control or the need to be right. It requires holding your tongue when you want to offer up the "better" solution and listening to your partner's point of view with the awareness that he or she could be right.

If you are in the habit of trying to impose your "rightness" on your partner's "wrongness," then you may need a gentle reminder from your partner when this happens. If you can accept this reminder without resentment and you truly want to change, ask your partner to speak up when you engage in black-and-white thinking so you become more aware of it.

Make it a practice to assume that you may NOT be right, or 100% right, and leave room for your partner's experience or point of view.

Put yourself in your partner's shoes.

An excellent way to implement the habit of acceptance is by putting yourself in your partner's position. How would you feel if you partner was constantly critical, frustrated, or disappointed in you? Think about the stress, unhappiness, shame, and guilt you would feel knowing your partner doesn't accept you as you are.

Of course, you want your partner to offer you love and acceptance without imposing his or her will on you or trying to change who you are. So offer this acceptance to your partner, even if it takes some time for your mind-set to catch up.

Sometimes we try to change our partners because we feel insecure about something within ourselves. Being kinder and more accepting of yourself and your own flaws can help dissolve the control you might want to impose on your partner.

Mindful Relationship Habit #6
Cherish Your Partner

In many traditional marriage vows, you will find the word "cherish" in a promise made between couples. "I promise to love, honor, and cherish you as long as we both shall live."

This is a lovely sentiment, but what does it really mean to cherish your partner, and why is it so important for your relationship?

According to *Merriam-Webster Dictionary*, cherish means "to hold dear," "feel or show affection for," "to keep or cultivate with care and affection," and "to entertain or harbor in the mind deeply and resolutely."

When you cherish your partner, you view him or her as a treasure, someone you value so highly and care for so tenderly that you would never want to say or do anything to cause pain or harm. You view your partner as the most special person in the world.

You may have cherished a material object in the past—a shiny new car, a family heirloom, or a prized garden. You took extra care to ensure the safety, protection, and maintenance of this thing. You stood back and enjoyed the satisfaction and fulfillment this thing gave you.

Says Gary L. Thomas, author of the book, *Cherish: The One Word That Changes Everything for Your Marriage*:

You don't put a Tiffany engagement ring in a shoebox. You don't frame a Rembrandt in a Popsicle stick frame. You wouldn't use a genuine George Washington autograph as a coaster.

The way we treat something acknowledges whether we cherish it or hold it with indifference or contempt. To truly cherish something is to go out of our way to show it off, protect it, and honor it. We want others to see and recognize and affirm the value that we see.

But of course, a material object doesn't talk back and push your hot buttons. It doesn't make demands or leave its dirty underwear on the floor. It's harder to cherish your love partner and maintain your ability to cultivate your relationship with care and affection.

But cherishing one another is a foundational part of a deeply satisfying, mindful relationship. Says Thomas, "Learning to truly cherish each other turns marriage from an obligation into a delight. It lifts marriage above a commitment to a precious priority."

When you cherish your spouse or partner, you show a willingness to put your partner first with a sense of loving devotion. You treat him or her with gentleness and provide an emotionally stable and nurturing environment. You hold your partner in the highest esteem, even when you experience minor irritations and frustrations.

When you cherish your partner, you also offer ongoing acceptance, a gentle understanding that no one is perfect, as we discussed in the previous habit. Your love and devotion for your partner trump any flaws or deficiencies.

To truly cherish your partner, you should also be willing to foster their growth and development—to give the emotional, moral, and spiritual support they require to continue to evolve and flourish as an individual throughout the marriage or relationship.

How to Develop This Habit

Cherishing your partner involves not only mentally embracing this ideal, but also initiating consistent daily actions to show your partner the respect and affection you feel.

In addition to practicing loving behaviors, you need to create an environment that fosters intimacy, emotional security, and personal growth for your partner.

This sounds like a tall order, but when you reflect on how much your partner means to you and how important his or her happiness is to your own, then you will *look for ways* to cherish your partner.

Most of the habits we outline in this book are acts of cherishing, but here are some specific ideas on habits that show your partner how much you cherish him or her.

Use a morning reminder.

Use a sticky note or iPhone reminder you see first thing in the morning (but that your partner *cannot* see) that reads, "How can I cherish my partner today?"

Use this reminder to brainstorm one or two specific things you can do to show your partner how much you cherish him or her. It may be tempting to roll over in bed and say to your partner, "I really cherish you," and call it a day. Loving words do show you honor your partner, but they have their limits. *Doing something* shows more effort, energy, and love.

Maybe it's bringing your spouse a cup of coffee in bed, taking over the morning routine with the kids, or surprising him at work with lunch. It could be asking your partner's opinion and really listening to it, or offering a head rub when you know she has had a stressful day.

Not only will your partner feel cherished, but you will also feel the joy of secretly planning and implementing your daily "cherish action."

Make frequent small (and occasional large) sacrifices for your partner.

When you cherish your partner, you desire to put them first as often as you can. It feels good to be selfless and generous with him or her. You take pleasure in your partner's pleasure.

We aren't suggesting you compromise yourself or become a doormat. Of course, there are times when you require boundaries or have to prioritize your own needs. We are talking about the small sacrifices that show the other person how much you care.

It could be offering him the last piece of cake or going to the movie she prefers. Maybe you clean up the kitchen even if it's your partner's turn. These small giving acts are a way of saying, "I love you, and I want you to be happy."

There also will be times when bigger sacrifices are called for. Maybe you agree to move for your spouse's job because you know it will make her happy, even though you don't want to leave your own job. Or you give up the vacation you've been planning because your partner wants a new car.

If there is a balance to these sacrifices, with both partners showing a fairly equal willingness to put the other's needs first, you will both discover a deeper sense of enrichment in your relationship than you thought possible.

Speak with kindness, tenderness, and warmth.

It is so easy for bitterness, or even contempt to sneak into our words when we speak to our partners. There is nothing that feels less like respect than a cutting remark, a sarcastic turn of phrase, or an icy tone. Even our nonverbal communication can be wounding, like eye-rolling, cold stares, and smirks.

There is no downside to speaking to your spouse with kindness. And certainly in everyday conversation, being aloof or businesslike doesn't do much to bring you and your partner closer. Instead, allow the warmth of your love for your partner to shine through your words and tone of voice.

Even during conflict, you can use a conciliatory tone and words of kindness. You can show through your words and tone your desire to reach a resolution and preserve the closeness between you. You can offer soft words even when a harsh response might be justifiable.

Think about the tender and loving way you might speak to a beloved child, and try to offer that same tenderness to your partner. We're not suggesting you talk down to your spouse, but rather that you adopt the same caring language you might offer a child.

Praise your partner in public.

Have you ever been out with another couple, and one partner criticizes or diminishes the other in front of you? Everyone laughs awkwardly and tries to move on, but you can see the hurt and betrayal in the wounded partner's eyes.

When partners cherish one another, they not only avoid demeaning each other in public, but rather they find ways to give praise. You want others to see the best qualities in your partner, and you make a point to offer words of affirmation and appreciative looks to your significant other in front of everyone.

You never feel like less of a man or woman by allowing your partner to shine and take the spotlight. It makes you feel happy to see him or her in the glow of other people's appreciation.

Ask your partner what being cherished means.

The best way to cherish your partner is to offer those things that make your partner feel cherished. Speaking with loving-kindness, making sacrifices, and offering public praise are all important, but only your partner knows what really feels special to him or her.

Talk with your partner about the importance of taking your relationship to the next level by cherishing one another. Ask what specific words and behaviors make him or her feel deeply cherished, then work on building these behaviors as new daily habits.

Once you experience the contentment, joy, and almost spiritual connection that comes from cherishing one another, you will find it easy to offer your partner what he or she desires to feel more cherished.

Mindful Relationship Habit #7
Touch Often

Do you and your partner touch each other often with affection? Do you make a habit of connecting physically by hugging, cuddling, kissing, and gently touching several times throughout the day?

If one or both of you isn't physically affectionate, or if you have developed an "affection deficiency" over time, this is a fundamental habit to focus on. Physical affection is so important that it's tied for the number one reason couples seek therapy, along with communication issues, according to research.

Studies have proven that physical affection correlates with general relationship satisfaction. In fact, a study published in *The American Journal of Family Therapy* states that partners involved in a romantic relationship feel more satisfied with their relationship when they are showing more physical affection toward each other. The more affection the respondents showed, the better the relationship.

Says Sean M. Horan PhD in an article for *Psychology Today*, "Specifically, we found, the frequency with which you expressed affection to and received affection from a partner was directly related to your commitment and satisfaction—and research documents that satisfaction and commitment are important, as they predict relational persistence over a 15-year period."

Conflict resolution also was generally found to be easier with more physical affection, like cuddling and holding, as affection helps to reduce stress by lowering cortisol levels. Though your first instinct might be to withdraw and withhold affection after conflict, the best thing you can do to mend fences and reconnect is to hug one another— or at least hold hands.

Physical affection between partners also can significantly lower systolic and diastolic blood pressure and increased heart rate. Hugging, cuddling, and kissing one another seems to increase levels of oxytocin, the "love hormone," which has been linked to social bonding. In women in particular, the oxytocin surge related to physical touch has a significant calming effect. Kissing was even shown to decrease cholesterol levels.

The amount of physical affection between couples predicts how much they love each other, as this study shows. In fact, increasing physical affection will increase feelings of love between the couple.

If you are someone who craves affection, developing this habit is natural for you. You readily offer hugs and cuddles and are willing to receive affection most any time. However, if you don't easily offer or receive physical affection, and it makes you uncomfortable, then you may find developing this habit a struggle.

If one partner needs more affection than the other, you can both find ways to get your needs met by figuring out a compromise. The partner who wants more affection may not get as much as he or she would like but with negotiation might get more than was previously offered. The partner who is less affectionate will need to make more of an effort to offer physical affection, knowing how important it is to the other partner.

If both partners are not the touchy types, or if your affection has dwindled over the years, it is still beneficial for all of the reasons previously stated to add more physical affection into your daily routine. You may discover over time that you enjoy this extra affection more than you thought you might.

The important thing is that you and your partner find a way to reach a workable arrangement about how much and what kind of affection you both desire, knowing that you want to please and show respect to each other.

How to Develop This Habit

Here are a few ways you can increase intimate touching with your partner:

Write down your affection needs.

Both partners should take five to ten minutes to write down his or her *ideal* physical affection desires (not necessarily what you are giving and receiving now). This list should include *the kind* of affection you like, *when* you want the affection, and *how often* you want it. For example, you might write something like this:

» **Hugging:** a long hug every day before work and when we both come home from work; a hug to make up after a conflict; a hug when I'm upset or worried; a surprise hug from behind a few times a week; a long hug if we've been apart for a few days.

» **Cuddling:** cuddling on the sofa every night when we watch TV; cuddling for at least fifteen minutes after sex; cuddling for a few minutes in bed before we fall asleep.

» **Kissing:** a kiss every morning before work and when we both come home from work; a surprise long kiss a couple of times a week; kissing as part of foreplay before sex.

» **Other touching:** a back rub or foot rub a few times a week when we are watching TV; holding hands as part of cuddling while watching TV.

» **Public affection:** put your arm around me or hold my hand when we are out with friends or family.

Discuss your list with your partner.

Take turns reading your lists to one another, and make notes about where you are in agreement about the type and amount of affection you both want.

Then the partner who needs less affection should read the other partner's list to see what additional gestures of affection can be offered. For example, the less affectionate partner might not like cuddling in bed at all but is willing to cuddle for five minutes before sleep as a loving gesture.

The less affectionate partner should write down everything he or she is willing to do to offer more affection to the other partner. So now you should have two lists—one that includes the affection you both want and another that includes the touch the less affectionate partner is willing to offer and how often he or she will offer it.

If the less affectionate partner asks for less cuddling or wants the other partner to back off of public affection, talk about a substitute behavior that can be offered instead. Maybe it's loving words, a warm smile, or a quick hand squeeze.

Make a master list.

Combine the two lists to create a master list of physical affection the two of you will offer one another. Review the list again to make sure you are both in agreement. You may need to make compromises to ensure each of you feels comfortable with the agreement.

Decide where you will start.

If you have several new affection habits you want to adopt, choose just one to start with—preferably one that you will repeat every day. It could be a long hug in the morning or a nightly five-minute cuddle before sleeping.

If you can't agree on where to start, flip a coin. Remember to offer the affection to one another graciously and with love. If you offer it with resentment or apathy, then it does more harm than good to your relationship.

Determine a time and a trigger.

Decide when you want to perform the affection habit and what will trigger the gesture. If the habit is cuddling in front of TV, then perhaps turning on the television is the trigger. If it's a hug in the morning, then gathering your keys or purse before work might be the trigger.

Remind one another.

The partner who is not as naturally affectionate may need a gentle reminder to follow through on the affection habit, especially if it's a habit that doesn't happen daily (like a back rub on Tuesdays and Thursdays, for example).

The goal is to remember to offer this affection without a reminder from your partner, so adding it to your calendar with a reminder set is a good idea. But in the beginning, be patient with one another as you try to establish the habit.

Offer less touch to the less affectionate partner.

If your partner has requested you not cuddle or touch as often and has made a specific suggestion about this, find a substitute behavior that works for both of you, as mentioned earlier. Find out what the less affectionate partner prefers, and try to offer that gesture instead when you would normally be more touchy.

Remember that some amount of physical affection is necessary for the health and happiness of your relationship. As the research suggests, the more affection between you, the happier your connection. It's worth the extra effort on the part of the partner who isn't as keen on affection to stretch a little and make room for a more physically affectionate connection.

Continue with more affection habits.

Once you feel the first habit has become automatic, go back to your list and decide on another form of physical affection you want to cultivate. You may find after igniting more physicality with the first habit that it's easier to be affectionate without having to work on it.

Try to connect physically a few times a day at least to experience the benefits that physical touch provides. Talk to each other in your weekly meetings about how this increased affection is impacting both of you and your relationship.

Mindful Relationship Habit #8
Connect and Engage Daily

Being regularly connected and engaged with one another as a couple is the foundation of a mindful relationship. It is a habit that requires daily attention, as it's so easy to become preoccupied with the daily stress of life, creating a slippery slope toward apathy and estrangement.

Too many relationships look like this:

> You begin the day in a hurry to get out the door to your jobs or other obligations. You may talk or text once or twice very briefly during the eight-hour day. You come home to more obligations and demands, like tending to kids, running errands, and preparing dinner. You eat a quick meal in front of the TV, clean the dishes, surf the net, or do a few more chores, then head to bed exhausted, having conversed very little with one another about anything meaningful.

Being connected and engaged means spending one-on-one time together daily—talking, discussing your hopes and dreams, and sharing your concerns of the day. It means being fully present with your partner when you are talking together, listening attentively without distraction or preoccupation. You must have this foundation of connectedness in place in order to work as a fully committed team.

If one or both of you is disconnecting in the relationship and not making daily time for one another, then right now is not too soon to recognize this problem and the potential it has for damaging your love, trust, and intimacy.

Says Dr. John Gottman in his book *The Seven Principles for Making Marriage Work*, "Our lab studies indicate that these emotionally distant couples do divorce—but they split after an average of 16 years ..." Disengagement is a slow-working poison that erodes the ties that bind you together.

Why is it that couples become disconnected and disengaged from one another? Why do they begin to pull apart and live more like roommates than true love partners?

Often jobs, children, and other life responsibilities get in the way of making time to spend together as a couple. We are so tired and overwhelmed that we put the one person who should be prioritized on the back burner.

Disengagement can also stem from feelings of boredom, hopelessness, or frustration within the relationship. It only takes one person to disengage for the poison to spread and infect the relationship. Eventually the person trying to engage and seeking engagement from the other will give up.

So what does full and loving engagement involve? Here are some of the ways you show engagement to one another:

> » understanding and embracing your partner's vulnerabilities, weaknesses, and pain

» helping and supporting your partner to grow beyond those weaknesses and feel safe and loved

» having a willingness to share your own vulnerabilities, weaknesses, and pain

» practicing active and reflective listening

» striving for emotionally mature communication and conflict resolution

» initiating physical and emotional presence on a daily basis

» showing physical affection and intimacy

» reconnecting through fun, play, and shared interests

» making proactive efforts to stay connected when physically separated

» consciously placing the relationship in high priority over work, hobbies, and other life distractions

» having a willingness and desire to grow as a person, to seek personal evolution, and to invite your partner to grow and share with you in this

» having a willingness to forgive and ask for forgiveness

Of course, much of the connection and engagement in a relationship is personal and specific to the two people involved. You know it when you feel it and see it. You remember how it felt at the beginning of the relationship when you were both deeply intertwined, and you can draw from those memories to find the ways you want to connect again.

How to Develop This Habit

Can a relationship come back from a period of disengagement? Yes, it is possible to reignite your closeness, learn to open up with one another, and engage in activities that will foster greater intimacy and connection.

The best place to begin with this habit is by assessing where you and your partner might be disconnecting or feeling apathetic in your relationship.

How disconnected have you become?

Respond to the following seventeen statements below to help you determine your level of disconnection:

1. My partner and I don't feel close anymore, and we don't know how to reconnect.

    ___Very True   ___Somewhat True   ___Rarely True

2. One or both of us feels bored in our relationship.

    ___Very True   ___Somewhat True   ___Rarely True

3. We are too busy to work on our relationship right now.

    ___Very True   ___Somewhat True   ___Rarely True

4. Talking with each other about problems feels useless because it doesn't seem to help.

    ___Very True   ___Somewhat True   ___Rarely True

5. We find ourselves spending more time at work, with the kids, watching TV, or on the computer than we do with each other.

___Very True ___Somewhat True ___Rarely True

6. We rarely call or text each other when we are apart.

___Very True ___Somewhat True ___Rarely True

7. We don't spend much time thinking about one another's needs.

___Very True ___Somewhat True ___Rarely True

8. We don't initiate deep and close conversation very often.

___Very True ___Somewhat True ___Rarely True

9. We are often distracted or disinterested when we do talk.

___Very True ___Somewhat True ___Rarely True

10. We have lost interest in sexual intimacy.

___Very True ___Somewhat True ___Rarely True

11. We would rather spend time with friends or family than with each other.

___Very True ___Somewhat True ___Rarely True

12. We don't initiate fun times or dates with each other very often.

___Very True ___Somewhat True ___Rarely True

13. We don't hug or touch each other much anymore.

___Very True ___Somewhat True ___Rarely True

14. We have little energy for working out conflict.

___Very True ___Somewhat True ___Rarely True

15. We don't socialize as a couple anymore.

___Very True   ___Somewhat True   ___Rarely True

16. We don't open up and share things like we used to.

___Very True   ___Somewhat True   ___Rarely True

17. It seems we are more like roommates than lovers.

___Very True   ___Somewhat True   ___Rarely True

Review your answers together.

Go over the answers you both gave for the 17 statements. Pay close special attention to those where you answered "very true" or "somewhat true." Make notes about where you and your partner are becoming distant and disengaged.

Ask yourself and each other why you think this is happening.

» Is it related to the demands and responsibilities of life?

» Have you just neglected to give the relationship the attention it needs?

» Is there something else more serious going on that is making you or your partner pull away?

(**Note:** If there is a serious reason causing the disengagement, like a conflict, infidelity, or addiction, consider working with a licensed couple's counselor to address this challenge.)

Decide where to begin reconnecting and engaging.

Discuss where you think you should reconnect with one another based on your answers to the previous questions. Sometimes it can be as simple as deciding to take a walk together every day or having some alone time without the kids at the end of the day.

You may need to reconnect physically by reigniting your sex life or increasing your physical affection. Maybe you need more date nights or time for fun and play within the relationship.

If the two of you are feeling really disconnected, start with something simple, like setting aside ten minutes to hold hands and share the events of the day. This isn't a time to discuss problems or concerns. It should be a positive bonding time where you both have the chance to talk and listen.

Take turns sharing while the other partner listens attentively without interruptions. You can ask questions or make comments after the other person has finished talking. (You'll read more about active listening in Habit #15.)

Choose a time, a place, and a trigger.

Determine when and how often you'll practice this reconnection habit. Beginning with a habit you can perform daily, like having a one-on-one planned conversation, will help you cement the habit.

Be specific by determining:

- » What time of day do you want to perform this habit, and how long do you want to engage in it?
- » What trigger will remind you to perform it?
- » Where is the best place to perform it to ensure you won't be distracted or interrupted?

Set up a reminder system.

In addition to your trigger, set up a reminder system to help you remember to perform the habit. You might put a reminder on your phone or post a reminder somewhere in your home where you will easily see it.

Continue connecting and engaging with more habits.

Be more mindful of one another throughout the day by connecting and engaging several times. These can be small touches, like a loving text or call in the middle of the day, as well as more significant ways of reconnecting.

Brainstorming ways to spend bonding time as a couple can be a fun and satisfying habit itself to work on together.

If you get stuck, you can try these ideas:

- » Go for a bike ride.
- » Look at old photos together.
- » See a funny movie.
- » Go camping.
- » Create a mixtape together.
- » Talk openly about your feelings.
- » Share dreams with each other.
- » Cuddle outside under a blanket.
- » Sit together in the park.
- » Take a long walk together.
- » Have a picnic.
- » Play Frisbee.

» Go swimming.

» Go grocery shopping.

» Take a road trip.

» Plan a party together.

» Go to the bookstore.

» Spend a day at the museum.

» Wash each other's cars.

» Take a personality test together.

» Go fishing.

» Write each other love letters.

» Go hiking.

» Take a moonlit walk.

» Make love in a new place.

» Write a poem and read it to each other.

» Eat dinner by candlelight.

» Go to a concert.

» Watch the sunrise together.

» Watch the sunset together.

» Go out dancing.

» Tell each other funny stories.

» Spend time at the beach.

» Take a ride through the countryside.

» Play a board game.

- » Give massages.
- » Volunteer at a charity event.
- » Take silly pictures.
- » Climb a jungle gym.
- » Enjoy each other's company.

Mindful Relationship Habit #9
Create Shared Rituals

The etymology of the word "ritual" dates back to the 1560s and relates to religious rites, observances, customs, or ceremonies. These sacred rituals involve prescribed traditions, actions, words, and objects to symbolize some element of a specific faith or doctrine.

Rituals have since evolved from solely religious activities to become part of our everyday lives, weaving their way into holidays, weddings, funerals, graduation ceremonies, and family gatherings. In the simplest form, a ritual is any practice or pattern of behavior regularly performed in a set manner.

Although modern-day rituals may or may not be religious, the sacredness of the ritual is maintained through the deep emotional, social, or familial connections made between the individuals involved.

Says ritual expert Donna Henes in an article for *The Huffington Post*, "A compelling urge to merge with the infinite, ritual reminds us of a larger, archetypal reality and invokes in us a visceral understanding of such universal paradigms as unity, continuity, connectivity, reverence, and awe."

With rituals, the medium itself is the message, as the events or actions involved communicate something important to those who understand their significance—in this case, the two of you.

Although couples often have little awareness of the relationship-nurturing function of their rituals, there is no better place to perform rituals than in your marriage or love partnership—this most important relationship in your life. Couple rituals help prevent the tendency for the relationship to run on autopilot, leading to apathy and disengagement.

Couple rituals help you:

- » anchor your emotions to a specific, established act
- » afford structure and significance to your interactions
- » build a positive emotional reservoir
- » enhance deeper intimacy and closeness within the ritualized activity
- » facilitate the entrance into a desired emotional state
- » foster security and trust
- » accomplish specific tasks together
- » fulfill needs for both predictability and novelty
- » solidify a strong shared identity, creating a feeling of being a "we"
- » make your life together more interesting, playful, and fun

All these benefits pay huge dividends for your relationship. They promote the happiness and longevity of the relationship by deepening intimacy, romance, friendship, commitment, and stability.

You and your partner likely have some rituals already established between you. Maybe you read out loud to one another in bed before going to sleep, or you have a practice of preparing and cooking a romantic dinner together on Friday nights. You may have established holiday rituals or special ceremonies to celebrate birthdays.

Sometimes a commonplace activity can evolve into a ritual when you realize it's taking on more significance in your lives. You might discover that your morning coffee together has become a meaningful way to start your day, or your occasional walks in nature have transformed into a sacred time to connect and talk.

The more rituals you and your partner establish together, the more you will bond. With rituals, you are creating a "couple bubble" in which you solidify your interdependence and prioritize your relationship by thinking in terms of "we" rather than "me."

How to Develop This Habits

Sit down together and make a list of all the small daily rituals you share as a couple, as well as the bigger occasions (like holidays) that you have rituals around.

Discuss what you like about these rituals, how they make you feel, and the purpose they serve in enhancing your relationship (e.g., they foster trust, build intimacy, help manage conflict). Are there any rituals you would like to change, enhance, or drop? Make notes about your answers.

Review events or activities you would like to ritualize.

Discuss some of the events or activities you do together now that feel rote, rushed, or sporadic that you might want to ritualize.

Perhaps you've gotten into a rut of eating dinner in front of the TV, but you would rather sit at the table, light candles, put on music, and make it a special occasion—at least a few times a week.

If you have chores or tasks that are boring or causing stress between you, think of ways you can work together and create a fun ritual that turns the chore into a vehicle for closeness and teamwork.

Make a list of these scenarios that have the potential for becoming a couple's ritual.

Brainstorm new rituals to work on together.

If you don't have many rituals in your relationship, spend some creative time together brainstorming ideas. These can be daily, weekly, monthly, or seasonal rituals. Put all of your ideas on paper, and then later you'll come back and decide which ones you want to add into your lives right now.

Need some ritual ideas to get started?

Here are some rituals to consider:

» Plan a monthly or quarterly weekend getaway for just the two of you.

» Cuddle in bed for five minutes in the morning before you both get up.

» Greet each other with a long hug and kiss at the end of every day.

» Plan your weekly meeting from Habit #1 in a special location, with a lit candle and soft music.

» Develop a daily mutual appreciation ritual.

» Leave each other hidden love notes every day.

» Practice a morning yoga routine together.

» Have a morning coffee and breakfast ritual.

» Make the bed together.

» Come up with a ritual for making up after an argument that includes touch, apologies, and words of affirmation.

» Have a regular date night, doing something new on each date.

» Celebrate small successes with a glass of champagne.

» Go on a Saturday morning bike ride.

» Go to bed at the same time and read together.

» Create a special lovemaking ritual.

» Have a set, daily check-in time when you are apart.

» Send each other selfies when you are apart.

» Take turns treating each other to a back rub or head rub.

» Find a special TV show or series you watch together.

» Create a weekly "holiday" you celebrate together.

» Develop private rituals around big holidays and birthdays.

» Learn a new skill or take a class together.

» Develop a special way you celebrate your anniversary.

» Create "special request" jars filled with loving actions you want your partner to offer you. Take turns picking one from your partner's jar and offering it.

» Have a photo taken together every year (or month) in the same location to chronicle your lives together.

Choose your first ritual to develop as a habit.

Start by choosing one ritual to work on and add into your schedules. This can be an action you already perform but want to ritualize or a brand-new ritual you develop from scratch.

Consider choosing a ritual that seems to fit your personalities and relationship and that adds a useful or needed benefit to your lives. Review the list of benefits to help you decide.

You want this ritual to be meaningful and special for both of you—not something that feels like a chore or obligation. So come up with something you both agree will be positive and fun (or beneficial).

To help you establish this ritual as a habit, choose one that you can do daily or at least several days a week.

Plan out the specifics of the ritual.

Talk to your partner to determine:

- » Exactly what will this ritual entail?
- » When and where do you want to do it?
- » Who initiates it?
- » How will it be done?

Hammer out all the details involved and write them down. Be creative and positive as you work on planning this ritual together. View this planning time as something fun and important for your relationship.

Create a trigger or reminder.

If the ritual is brand new, you will need to attach it to a trigger to help you remember to do it. You may also want to set up other reminders so you don't forget when you first begin.

If one of you is better at remembering the ritual than the other, that's fine. That person can initiate the ritual as long as the other person willingly jumps in and participates fully.

Discuss your ritual and what might need to change.

You may decide to alter elements of the ritual to suit your needs or desires. Maybe the time isn't working, you didn't think through part of it, or you feel an important action is missing. At the end of each week, discuss your ritual and how you both think it is going.

Remember to be fully present and engaged in whatever ritual you are trying to establish as a habit. This effort shouldn't feel difficult—like you're trying to develop a running or dieting habit, which can be intimidating. You should both enjoy this habit and want to take the time to make it a regular part of your day.

Slowly add more rituals.

After a few weeks, once you have refined and solidified your first ritual, slowly add more small rituals to your lives. You may decide on rituals that happen less frequently or just on holidays or special occasions.

For these, having a trigger won't help you. You'll need to put the date(s) on your calendars, and also set a time in advance to plan out what you need to do to follow through on the ritual. It's easy to forget your plans to do something special for a birthday or holiday if you don't prepare in advance and set up reminders.

Don't overwhelm yourselves by creating too many rituals. If you do, the ones you already have will begin to lose their significance. Have a handful of rituals you plan, and remember that many small rituals will occur spontaneously between you, especially now that you know how important they are to your relationship.

Mindful Relationship Habit #10
Practice Vulnerability

Do you feel free and comfortable being fully yourself with your partner?

Can you share your deepest secrets, most embarrassing mistakes, and most painful insecurities?

Can you be completely authentic and open, revealing your most intimate dreams and longings, secure in the knowledge that you won't be ridiculed or rejected but instead embraced?

Can you be completely vulnerable and exposed without the anxiety that your partner will stop loving you or will judge you harshly?

Unfortunately, most of us have been trained from an early age not to be vulnerable, not to talk about our weaknesses or fears. We've learned the painful lesson of opening our hearts, telling our truths, and showing our frailties, only to have our hearts broken and our weaknesses disparaged.

We've learned to hold back, to pretend to be someone else, to protect our hearts. We've learned that the best defense against pain is a good offense. So we build brick walls. We hold ourselves at arm's length. We show only our best sides. Of course, it's exhausting and stressful maintaining this pretense. It takes a lot of energy to be something you're not.

Holding back does protect you from emotional pain in the short term. But in the long run it wreaks havoc on your relationship. Without vulnerability in your relationship, intimacy will wither and die, like a flower that never develops deep roots.

This kind of openness should become easier over time and with practice as you both feel safer in the knowledge that you are cherished no matter what. But developing this security requires that you routinely reveal yourself to your partner and expose your feelings rather than hiding them or stuffing them.

It requires letting down your guard and inviting your partner into your inner world through regular dialogue as well as a mutual regard for one another's sense of emotional safety and respect.

There are nine reasons why vulnerability and the ability to communicate freely are essential for intimacy in your relationship:

1. Vulnerability reveals the complete person you are.

When you are able to show yourself fully to your partner, you experience the joy and freedom of being fully yourself. And your partner benefits from knowing all of you, not just the glossed-over, superficial parts of you.

You both enjoy the depths and intricacies of all aspects of each other—the good, the bad, and the ugly. There is beauty and healing in being known so completely by someone you love and who loves you.

2. Vulnerability fosters trust.

As you reveal yourself to your partner in deep conversations, and they respond with respect, love, and dignity, your trust in your partner expands. As you reveal more of yourself, you invite your partner to be vulnerable as well.

You give them the courage to show the hidden or shameful parts of themselves. Both of you experience the security and peace of having the other's back and knowing you are still loved and respected.

3. Being vulnerable with one another invites growth.

It allows you to reflect honestly on your true self within the safe harbor of a trusting relationship. You can assess changes you need to make and the person you want to become without taking a blow to your self-esteem.

Self-honesty is critical to living authentically, which in turn opens doors to untapped potential within yourself. A loving, mindful partner provides a comforting space in which to evolve and grow, minimizing the pain that transformation often creates.

4. Vulnerable conversations build your confidence.

As you practice expressing your feelings, revealing your flaws, and admitting your fears, you see that the practice of vulnerability doesn't diminish you but actually strengthens you.

You realize you can expose yourself *without* becoming less of a person. You are bolstered by your ability to stand firm in your own truth and acknowledge your flaws and regrets. They are part of who you are and what has brought you to this place in life. A loving, mindful partner will celebrate all of who you are and how you are becoming.

5. Vulnerability heals wounds.

All healing begins with acknowledgment, acceptance, and awareness. When you are real about your pain or fear, rather than trying to run from it or hide it, you purge yourself of the blocked feelings and the stress of trying to pretend or ignore.

By putting things out in the open with your partner, you allow the light of truth to ignite the healing process.

6. Vulnerability creates bonding.

All of us have areas of ourselves we fear revealing or sharing with another, even our partner. We all have regrets, shameful feelings, and self-doubt. When you're able to open up about these with the most important person in your life, you connect even more deeply with *their* humanness.

You allow your partner to see that you are just like him or her, that you share common feelings and fears. This bonds you closer to each other as you recognize that you aren't alone in your humanness.

7. Sharing in a vulnerable way deepens your love.

Being vulnerable means you can express your deepest feelings and share love on a more profound level. You can be tender, affectionate, silly, emotional, and passionate in ways that elevate your relationship to an almost spiritual experience.

Rather than growing bored with each other, your vulnerability allows you to reveal more and more layers of yourselves over the years. Your relationship becomes an exciting adventure of mutual exploration that makes your love deeper and stronger.

8. Vulnerability makes you more attractive and interesting.

Nothing is more appealing than authenticity. By being fully yourself and confidently accepting your good and bad qualities, you become more interesting and attractive to your partner.

Your ability to express yourself openly and acknowledge your flaws makes your partner feel safe and confident around you as well.

9. Vulnerability teaches you comfort with uncertainty.

When we are vulnerable, we don't always know how our partner will respond to us. We take a huge risk by putting ourselves out there. This uncertainty causes discomfort and anxiety.

By practicing vulnerable sharing, you grow accustomed to uncertainty and can tolerate the unpleasant feelings it causes, especially if your partner responds with love and kindness. You can use this new toughness to cope with other areas of risk in your life that can stretch you and expand opportunities for growth.

As bestselling author and vulnerability expert Brené Brown reminds in her book *The Gifts of Imperfection*, "Owning our story can be hard but not nearly as difficult as spending our lives running from it. Embracing our vulnerabilities is risky but not nearly as dangerous as giving up on love and belonging and joy—the experiences that make us the most vulnerable. Only when we are brave enough to explore the darkness will we discover the infinite power of our light."

How to Develop This Habit

To develop the habit of being more vulnerable with one another, it helps to have an idea of how comfortable you are with vulnerability right now. This awareness will give you a starting point for working on more vulnerable talking and listening.

Respond to the following 21 statements about being vulnerable with your partner. For any statement to which you answer, "Somewhat true" or "Rarely true," write down the problem or reason why you answered as you did.

1. My partner is emotionally available to me most of the time.

   ___Very true   ___Mostly true   ___Somewhat true   ___Rarely true

2. When I need to share something, my partner prioritizes me and listens.

   ___Very true   ___Mostly true   ___Somewhat true   ___Rarely true

3. I feel comfortable sharing my insecurities with my partner.

   ___Very true   ___Mostly true   ___Somewhat true   ___Rarely true

4. I feel comfortable sharing my hopes and dreams with my partner.

   ___Very true   ___Mostly true   ___Somewhat true   ___Rarely true

5. I feel comfortable crying in front of my partner.

   ___Very true   ___Mostly true   ___Somewhat true   ___Rarely true

6. I feel my partner loves and accepts me for who I am, flaws and all.

   ___Very true   ___Mostly true   ___Somewhat true   ___Rarely true

7. There is no topic that is off-limits with my partner.

___Very true   ___Mostly true   ___Somewhat true   ___Rarely true

8. My partner is the first person I turn to when I'm feeling upset or afraid.

___Very true   ___Mostly true   ___Somewhat true   ___Rarely true

9. When I share something with my partner, I feel heard and understood.

___Very true   ___Mostly true   ___Somewhat true   ___Rarely true

10. My partner and I have regular (daily or weekly) deep and meaningful conversations.

___Very true   ___Mostly true   ___Somewhat true   ___Rarely true

11. My partner knows more about me than anyone.

___Very true   ___Mostly true   __ Somewhat true   ___Rarely true

12. I completely trust that my partner will protect me emotionally.

___Very true   ___Mostly true   ___Somewhat true   ___Rarely true

13. My partner never tries to shame me about what I share with him/her.

___Very true   ___Mostly true   ___Somewhat true   ___Rarely true

14. I can talk openly about my sexual needs with my partner.

___Very true   ___Mostly true   ___Somewhat true   ___Rarely true

15. I can initiate sex or sexual activities without fear, shame, or anxiety.

___Very true   ___Mostly true   ___Somewhat true   ___Rarely true

16. I can talk openly about my emotional needs with my partner.

___Very true   ___Mostly true   ___Somewhat true   ___Rarely true

17. I never fear being rejected by my partner.

___Very true   ___Mostly true   ___Somewhat true   ___Rarely true

18. When my partner and I disagree or have conflict, I can express myself without fear.

___Very true   ___Mostly true   ___Somewhat true   ___Rarely true

19. My partner can read my emotions and expressions and know when we need to talk.

___Very true   ___Mostly true   ___Somewhat true   ___Rarely true

20. My partner makes it easy to be vulnerable.

___Very true   ___Mostly true   ___Somewhat true   ___Rarely true

21. Because of the safeness in our relationship, I feel more self-confident.

___Very true   ___Mostly true   ___Somewhat true   ___Rarely true

Review your answers and comments with each other.

Once you respond to the statements and make notes, sit down together and discuss the areas in which you both feel uncomfortable or unable to be vulnerable and open. Do you feel this way because of your own reticence to be vulnerable or because of the way your partner has reacted or responded in the past?

Generally speaking, men are more conditioned to be emotionally distant and less open about their weaknesses and insecurities than women. Being "macho" and in control is venerated in our culture and considered a sign of strength. Talking about feelings and fears might be deeply uncomfortable if you were raised to "man up" and hold it in.

If this is the case for you, you need to be particularly aware of letting down these walls with your spouse or partner and allow yourself to be vulnerable so that intimacy can flourish. Keeping your partner at arm's distance will eventually drive her away.

Whether you are a man or woman, if your partner's vulnerabilities make you uncomfortable or irritated, you'll need to manage and eventually transform these feelings by practicing more empathy, which we outline in Habit #16. Putting yourself in your partner's shoes is the best way to accept and love him or her without judgment.

Consider where you need to be a more open and vulnerable communicator, as well as how you can be a more loving, accepting, nonjudgmental listener to your partner's vulnerabilities. These areas are where your habit work should begin.

Set a time to share something vulnerable with your partner.

After you have explored and discussed how and why you are holding back and not being vulnerable, choose a time to share something vulnerable with one another. A good time might be during your weekly meeting or another calm time when you won't be distracted or interrupted by others.

This is a habit you may want to practice just once a week initially, as it can sometimes stir up intense emotions to reveal or share something uncomfortable or embarrassing. Working on this habit daily might be too intense.

As with other variable habits, you'll need to set up a reminder system to help you remember to practice this habit.

Choose a topic to share.

If you aren't in the practice of being open and vulnerable with one another, you may want to start with a safer topic. If you have a long-held big secret, and you're uncertain how your partner will react, you might want to save that conversation until you feel more secure and confident in sharing openly.

Some topics to consider include:

» an insecurity you have

» a past wound

» a failure or mistake you've made

» a dream or goal you haven't expressed

» a sexual fantasy

» a worry or concern about your abilities

» a fear or phobia

» an embarrassing experience

» a feeling or opinion you deem as inappropriate or wrong

» a weakness you have

» a lie you have told or continue to tell

» a situation where you've acted against your integrity

» a time you lost your temper

» a regret you hold onto

» a mental health issue that you suppress (e.g., low self-esteem, anxiety, or depression)

As the listener, invite full disclosure.

Each partner will practice sharing and being the listener. That means each of you needs to make the other feel safe, heard, and accepted as you listen and respond to what has been shared.

Accepting the gift of your partner's vulnerability means you listen actively (as outlined in Habit #15), and you offer compassion (if required), acknowledgment, acceptance, support, affection, and love. If invited, you can offer feedback or ideas, as long as they are not critical, defensive, or judgmental.

You may feel disappointed, embarrassed, uncomfortable, irritated, or threatened by your partner's vulnerable sharing. If your partner is revealing a lapse in character or a sexual fantasy that you find off-putting, it's only human to have your own reactions and emotions about the information.

But … it's important in the moment of vulnerable sharing that your first reaction isn't to shame, blame, or criticize. Instead, make your partner feel safe, and reinforce your love for him or her. Your reactions and facial expressions must remain calm and composed, even if you are churning on the inside.

Here are some steps to follow as the listener:

» Begin by saying to your partner something like this: "I want to know you fully and completely. You are safe talking to me because I will always love you."

» Sit close to your partner, hold his or her hand, and make eye contact.

» Listen attentively without becoming distracted or interrupting your partner. Offer visual encouragement for your partner to continue by nodding, squeezing his or her hand, or smiling with love.

» When your partner stops talking, ask if there is more he or she needs to say to feel completely unburdened or to clarify any points. If so, continue to listen attentively.

» Once your partner is done, thank him or her for being so open and vulnerable with you. If the topic was difficult or emotional, acknowledge that you know how hard it must have been to share it and how hard it was to keep it inside for so long.

» Confirm your commitment and feelings for your partner (even if you were upset by the information) by saying something like, "I love you so much, and I am here for you. We are a team."

» Ask your partner, "What do you need from me right now?" It may just be a listening ear, a hug, and the knowledge that you understand and accept him or her. Or it may be your partner needs forgiveness, support, feedback, or some action on your part.

» If you can offer your partner what he or she needs in the moment, offer it right away. If you can't or you're uncertain of your own feelings, offer an alternative or say something to your partner like, "I hear what you need, and I'd like to take some time to consider your request. I love you, and I'll come back to you about this soon."

As the speaker, consider the deeper revelations.

Before you speak, consider in advance what you want to share and the deeper emotions or needs behind the topic you want to reveal to your partner.

For example, you may share an embarrassing situation at work when you didn't have a project completed as the client expected. But the deeper emotions you're experiencing might be feelings of inadequacy or low self-esteem.

If you share a sexual fantasy, perhaps you have a deeper longing or emotional need you want met through the fantasy.

By revealing the emotions behind the surface feelings, you open yourself fully to your partner, giving him or her an understanding of your inner world, which is far more complex and "real" than anything you generally show to others.

Here are some steps to follow as the speaker:

» After your partner affirms that you are safe revealing yourself, begin by telling the story or relaying the information. "I had a situation at work that was really embarrassing." "I have a fantasy I've never shared with you before." "I have an emotional issue I haven't told you about."

» Have faith that your partner is true to his or her word and won't judge or criticize you. Then elaborate on the details of the situation, being fully truthful and detailed, not withholding information out of fear, discomfort, or shame.

» Once you share the details, reveal any deeper feelings. "I'm really concerned my boss will see me as inadequate." "I need to feel more desirable and sexy." "I'm afraid you won't love me if you know how depressed I am."

» Tell your partner what you need from him or her. "I need you to hug me for a few minutes." "I'd like you to be willing to try out my fantasy." "I need your assurance that you'll stick with me through this depression."

» Thank your partner for listening and making you feel safe to express yourself openly.

» If you want your partner's feedback, ask him or her to share what they think. This feedback should be offered gently and with love and compassion. This isn't the time for your partner to correct your behavior or negate your opinion.

Regroup and discuss your reactions and feelings.

After you have both had a chance to share, being vulnerable and listening to one another, circle back to discuss the exercise:

» How did it feel to be vulnerable with your partner?

» Did you feel safe and accepted by your partner?

» How did it feel listening to your partner being vulnerable?

» Do you feel closer to one another having shared openly?

» Is there anything more you need from your partner as the listener?

» As a result of sharing, is there more that needs to be discussed between the two of you related to the topics brought up?

Try to catch yourself building walls or shutting your partner out.

During your daily life together, become more aware of ways in which you resist being vulnerable with your partner. Notice times when you hide your emotions or pretend everything is okay when it really isn't.

Practice letting your partner see the "real" you as often as possible, and invite him or her into your emotional world, even when it isn't attractive or positive.

Within the safety of your partner's acceptance and love, your wounded places will heal, and you will feel liberated to be who you are with self-compassion and confidence.

Mindful Relationship Habit #11
Become an Expert on Your Partner

Have you ever been to a restaurant and seen a couple sitting a few tables away and they're barely speak to one another during the entire meal?

They eat their food as though they are sitting alone at the kitchen table, looking anywhere but at their partner. There's no laughter and very little conversation. In fact, they seem like two uncomfortable strangers.

If they can't interact while sitting across from each other in a public place, you wonder how much more disconnected they are in the privacy of their home.

As a marriage or relationship gets past the honeymoon phase, couples tend to fall into a sad pattern of inattention to the details of one another's lives. They neglect to show attention to their partner's thoughts, interests, dreams, likes, dislikes, and feelings. They believe they know everything there is to know about one another, so they stop being inquisitive and curious.

However, mindful couples make it a point to become intimately familiar with each other's worlds on an ongoing basis. They recognize that their partner is a deep and ever-evolving being to be explored and appreciated. They understand that people continue to grow and change, and they want to share in that growth with one another.

When you become an expert on your partner, you might know his favorite sports shows on TV. He knows exactly how you like your coffee because he pays attention. You both make time to ask about each other's day and to discuss what's on your mind. But becoming an expert involves more than just these daily preferences and activities. It involves exploring your inner worlds as well.

She remembers the painful memories of your childhood that still cause you to suffer, and she is there for you without you having to ask. He asks you probing questions about the class you are taking, knowing how important it is to you. You never tease him about those few extra pounds because you know he feels insecure about his weight.

Being genuinely curious and learning more about one another doesn't just improve your communication. It also protects your relationship from the inevitable storms and difficulties you will face as a couple.

When a couple is keenly aware of what each partner thinks and feels, they are less likely to be thrown for a loop when challenges occur. For example, when a couple has their first child, it creates a huge change in their lives, adding more demands with less sleep.

Couples who know each other well and communicate often about their thoughts, needs, and feelings are much less likely to experience relationship unhappiness during this time of upheaval when a baby enters their lives, according to research by marriage expert John Gottman.

Becoming an expert on your partner also fosters intimacy, compassion, mutual interests, novelty, and admiration. If your partner dreams of learning to sail, you might be inspired to join him in that dream, creating another avenue for companionship, learning, and fun.

If you inquire about your partner's anxiety related to her new job, you can be there to support and strengthen her in a way that best helps her. When you are curious about your partner's childhood, you'll have a better understanding of his emotional reactions and motivations.

The more you learn about each other, the deeper and more connected your relationship will grow. And because all of us continue to change and evolve over time, this mutual learning process is a lifetime endeavor. You can encourage, inspire, support, and motivate one another as you share your inner worlds year after year.

Rather than allowing yourselves to drift into separate corners over time, assuming that there's nothing left to know about each other, you can continue to unfold and reveal the depths of yourselves.

Does this mean you need to share or hear everything? If there are certain things you don't want to hear, like the details about your spouse's past lovers, that's understandable. Or if you don't want to mention that time you cheated on a test in high school, no harm done.

You can create appropriate boundaries around sharing, as long as you aren't hiding something significant or lying to your partner. But keep the door open to any kind of sharing that gives you more insight and understanding of one another as you grow through your lives.

How to Develop This Habit

Schedule a regular time to talk for 15 to 30 minutes when you won't be interrupted or distracted. Maybe it's just before bed or at the end of the evening meal. As you've done with other habits, establish a trigger and reminder system so you don't forget to follow through.

Hopefully, you will enjoy these exploratory conversations so much that they easily become part of your daily routine. You will find many occasions throughout the day to be curious and interested in your partner if you pay attention.

If you think of your partner as someone exceedingly fascinating, with a treasure trove of uniqueness to explore, then you'll find yourself looking for ways to become more engaged in his or her life.

Discover how well you currently know your partner.

Before you begin working on this habit, assess your current knowledge of your partner to see how well you know him or her.

Answer the following questions, writing down your answers in a journal or notebook. Then review your answers with your partner to see how many you answered correctly. With just this exercise, you'll be surprised at how much you learn about your partner.

Here is a list of potential questions you could ask:

1. What is stressing out your partner most right now?
2. How does your partner spend most of his/her time?
3. Who was your partner's closest childhood friend?
4. What are some things on your partner's bucket list?
5. What is your partner's favorite music?
6. What is one of the most pivotal moments in your partner's life?
7. What does your partner feel the most insecure about?
8. What would your partner do with the money if he/she won the lottery?

9. What is your partner's favorite meal?

10. What kind of books does your partner like?

11. What is one of your partner's sexual fantasies?

12. What is your partner's most painful life experience?

13. What kind of work would your partner like to do if he/she wasn't in this current job?

14. What is your partner's biggest life regret?

15. What was your partner wearing when you first met?

16. Where was your partner born?

17. What is your partner's favorite leisure activity?

18. What is your partner's favorite restaurant?

19. Who is your partner's current best friend?

20. What does your partner eat for breakfast most mornings?

21. What is one of your partner's main life goals?

22. What is something your partner doesn't like about himself/herself?

23. What is your partner most proud of?

24. Which member of your partner's extended family is he/she closest to?

25. What does your partner think about the most?

26. What is one of your partner's happiest childhood memories?

27. What are your partner's religious or spiritual beliefs?

28. How does your partner feel around his/her parents?

29. What does your partner value most in life?

30. What kind of gift would your partner love to receive?

31. What does your partner prefer to do on New Year's Eve?

32. What is your partner's favorite vacation spot?

33. What does your partner love most about you?

34. How does your partner feel about surprise birthday parties for him/her?

35. What does your partner need most from you in your relationship?

Consider what you want to discuss and learn.

There is an endless array of topics to discuss to learn more about one another. You'll be surprised at how much you really don't know about your partner once you begin talking and asking questions. Here are some ideas to help you:

- » Share the events of your day, the people you encountered, and how they impacted you.

- » Share your emotions, shifting moods, shameful or embarrassing feelings, and deepest fears.

- » Share stories about your childhood, your past loves, your friends, your parents, your travels, your jobs, and your life experiences.

- » Discuss books, podcasts, movies, current affairs, politics, your religious beliefs, your hopes and dreams, your life regrets, and your favorite memories.

- » Become so curious and intrigued by your partner that you never run out of questions, as though you are a detective trying to gather every detail. If you need additional ideas for questions that can help you improve your relationship and learn about one another, consider going through Barrie's book 201 Relationship Questions.

Provide a safe environment for sharing.

The key to success with this habit is to give one another a safe environment in which to share anything without fear of judgment, derision, teasing, or shaming, as we discussed in Habit #10 on vulnerability. You both want the freedom to share openly, offering the positive and not-so-positive parts of your inner worlds.

Neither of you should shame, tease, deride, or criticize the other during these conversations, even if you learn something unexpected or surprising. You want to encourage open and empathic communication that leads to deeper intimacy.

Find ways to expand your growth together.

As you learn more about one another, you will encounter opportunities for exploration, growth, and learning as a couple. Take full advantage of these opportunities as an upward call for your relationship and your own personal growth.

For example, if one of you becomes interested in meditation, you might go on a meditation retreat together as a couple or choose to meditate together every morning. If your partner has strong and well-researched political beliefs, this may inspire you to explore your own beliefs and what really matters to you as a citizen of the world.

Don't just listen and nod as you learn about each other. Let your partner's experiences, beliefs, interests, and opinions serve as a springboard for pursuing a fuller, richer experience of life together.

Mindful Relationship Habit #12
Embrace Your Love Languages

It's natural to assume that what makes you feel loved and happy is what will make your partner feel loved and happy. But the truth is, if you are making a special effort to express your love in ways that feel good for you, you may be missing the mark with your partner.

Do you really know what makes your partner feel loved, cherished, and happy in your relationship? If you haven't asked directly (or been told directly), your genuine efforts might not be having the desired effect.

One of the most fundamental aspects of a mindful, intimate connection with one another is expressing and offering what author and relationship expert Dr. Gary Chapman calls your "love languages."

You and your partner should be aware of your own love languages, and you should be willing to show love in the way your partner receives it. Without this understanding, you might end up feeling resentful that your needs aren't being met or frustrated that your loving efforts with your partner are unappreciated.

In his bestselling book, *The 5 Love Languages: The Secret to Love that Lasts*, Gary Chapman outlines five ways that people express and experience love. Over his 30 plus years of counseling couples, Dr. Chapman has noticed specific patterns in the way partners communicate—and it turns out that most of us express and interpret love in the same five ways, according to his observations.

These include:

» words of affirmation

» quality time

» gift giving

» acts of service

» physical touch

Chapman asserts that each of us has a primary and secondary love language that is revealed in the way we show love to others. By offering our own love language to our partner, we are actually revealing *our* deepest needs within the relationship—but not necessarily our partner's.

Observe how your partner shows love to you, and analyze what he or she complains about within the relationship, and you will better understand what your partner needs from you.

If your partner is especially affectionate with you, it reveals that he or she craves physical affection *from you*. Or if she complains about how bored and lonely she feels, your partner might need more quality time with you.

Since we all don't have the same love languages as our partners, we can easily misinterpret or neglect to understand how to give our partners what they most need. Asking your partner directly what he or she most wants and needs to feel loved and cherished is the best way to be clear.

By asking and then offering words and actions to support your partner's love languages, you tear down many of the barriers that undermine the closeness you both want to share.

Let's review each one of these five love languages and what they mean:

1. Words of affirmation

According to Dr. Chapman, one way to express love emotionally is to use words that affirm, validate, and build up your partner. Verbal compliments, or words of appreciation, are extremely powerful communicators of your love.

They should be expressed in simple, straightforward statements of affirmation, like:

You look so beautiful tonight.

I'm always so happy to see you when you come home.

I am amazed by your integrity.

You are the most important person in the world to me.

One of the best ways you can offer words of affirmation is by expressing your respect and admiration for your partner. It shows how much you love the unique individual that your partner is.

Positive, loving words hold real value for those who prioritize this love language. So remember that negative or insulting comments cut deep—and won't be easily forgotten.

2. Quality time

This love language is all about giving your partner your undivided attention, which makes him or her feel loved and comforted. But sitting together watching television or surfing the net doesn't count as quality time.

Says Dr. Chapman, "What I mean is sitting on the couch with the TV off, looking at each other and talking, devices put away, giving each other your undivided attention. It means taking a walk, just the two of you, or going out to eat and looking at each other and talking."

We are all pulled in different directions by competing forces and responsibilities, and our time is so valuable. Be sure you prioritize your quality-time-loving spouse in your busy life by setting apart some daily hours just for him or her.

3. Gift giving

For some people, receiving gifts, visible symbols of love, makes them feel deeply appreciated and cherished.

A physical gift is something you can hold in your hand. It represents that your partner was thinking of you and made an effort for you. The gift itself is a symbol of that thought, but it doesn't have to be expensive or elaborate.

What is most important is the thought behind the gift and the feelings of love it represents.

4. Acts of service

With this love language, you do things you know your partner would like you to do; you seek to please him or her through serving.

Actions like doing your partner's laundry, setting the table, getting the tires rotated, cleaning the house, and running errands are all acts of service that show you care for your partner.

These actions require thought, planning, time, effort, and energy. If done with a generous spirit, they are true expressions of love.

This particular love language also requires a willingness to overcome stereotypes so you can express your feelings more effectively through acts of service. There is no reason a man can't prepare a meal or a woman can't mow the grass. If your spouse's love language is acts of service, then remember, what you do for him or her says, "I love you," louder than words.

5. Physical touch

If this is your love language, nothing feels more loving and affirming than your partner's touch.

These expressions through touch aren't just meant for the bedroom—nonsexual physical connections, like handholding, kissing, or cuddling are a big part of this love language.

Someone whose love language is physical touch will feel empty and disconnected without enough touching. Touch makes them feel secure in the love of their partner.

If you didn't grow up in an affectionate family, you may find it difficult to express your love this way. But if this is your partner's love language, you will need to learn exactly the kind of touch he or she desires and offer it more often.

Once you and your partner are aware of each other's love languages, your goal is to offer your partner more of what he or she needs to feel adored and cherished in the relationship. You may need to develop some new habits during your day to offer your partner what he or she needs.

One thing to remember—because you or your partner favor a particular love language, you shouldn't stop expressing the other love languages. According to Chapman, even though we tend to favor one language more than the others, we still enjoy expressions of the other languages as well.

How to Develop This Habit

To learn your own love language and your partner's, take Dr. Chapman's assessment to find out your primary and secondary love languages. You can downloading it as a PDF (or copy the link in your browser) and complete the assessment.

Your highest score will be your primary love language. Your second highest score will be your secondary love language. Once you know your own primary and secondary love languages, discuss them with your partner and learn what your partner's love languages are.

Discuss how you want your love languages expressed.

Now that you know your own love languages, write down a list of specific actions, words, and behaviors you would like your partner to use to express your love language.

For example, if physical touch is your love language, you might write down that you want more cuddling in bed, a back rub at night, or more hand holding. If you are an acts of service person, you might want your partner to surprise you by handling a certain chore or bringing you breakfast in bed once a week.

Select one love language behavior for your partner.

Once you've completed your lists, choose just one love language action or behavior to begin with that you want your partner to offer. Decide how often you want the action to be expressed and the time of day you want it.

You might choose a behavior that can be offered daily for this first habit. Practicing a consistent, daily action helps your partner develop the habit of offering it to you.

For example, you might request a back rub from your partner for ten minutes just before turning out the light, or you could ask your partner to handle making the bed every day before he or she goes to work. These are behaviors that can be offered daily at the same time with a regular trigger.

Ultimately, you want to meet your partner's love language needs spontaneously and creatively, without relying on a habit trigger or planning it for a certain time of day. But for now, just begin with one new love language behavior to get the ball rolling.

Offer the love language habit with love.

It won't feel like you are sincere in your efforts if you offer the requested behavior with resentment or passivity. The love language action should be offered graciously and wholeheartedly, showing your partner that you are truly pleased to be pleasing him or her.

Reflect on the person you were when you and your partner were first dating. Back in those early days, you would have been thrilled to offer this act of love to your partner. Draw from these memories and try to re-create the feelings you had then.

Make sure your trigger for this action is strong enough that you remember to act on it. You may need other reminders in the beginning to help you follow through. For this habit, it's better if you don't rely on your partner to remind you, as your forgetfulness can make your partner feel you aren't truly invested in meeting his or her needs.

Add more love language actions to your day.

As this first habit becomes more cemented, add another love language habit to your day. Look at your partner's list of desired love language behaviors and choose another one that you can perform regularly with a daily trigger.

However, you might decide to go for a more organic approach and look for opportunities throughout the day to express your partner's love language. Too many scheduled love habits might begin to feel rote and rehearsed for both you and your partner. Relying on the element of surprise in meeting your partner's needs can feel more genuine and caring.

Performing "variable" habits is harder because there is no daily consistency or set trigger built into the habit. But there are some habits that just don't work as well on a scheduled routine, and love language habits fit this bill.

The trick is remembering to look for natural opportunities to offer the love language behaviors and to act on them. You might put small and cryptic reminders around your house to trigger you to do something loving that you know your partner will like.

You don't need a big sign on the refrigerator that says, "Do something nice for Sue." Your partner doesn't need to see what you're up to. A rubber band on a doorknob or an item put in an unusual place can trigger you without alerting your spouse.

Make a game of it.

To keep this habit fun, brainstorm creative ways you can express your partner's love language. Rather than offering the traditional back rub to your physical-touch-loving spouse, offer to wash her hair with a luxurious shampoo and dry it for her.

Instead of telling your words-of-affirmation partner how much you love and appreciate him, write him a poem and read it in front of the entire family.

Look for new ways every day to surprise and delight your partner so that he or she is charmed and thrilled by your loving behavior. What better way to spark your creativity and personal joy than to come up with endless ways to show love to your lover.

Mindful Relationship Habit #13
Heal Hurts Quickly

Barrie once knew a couple that would allow arguments to drag on for days and days. The initial verbal battle might last just a few hours, but the aftereffects had a very long shelf life.

The couple wouldn't continue actively squabbling, but they would just stop speaking to one another unless absolutely necessary. They would move around each other in the house, sit silently at dinner, and go to bed without talking or resolving anything. For *days* this would go on!

As they stewed in their resentments, it became increasingly difficult to talk about their feelings, reach a resolution, and heal the wounds inflicted from the initial argument. Eventually, they would grow tired of not talking and would move on as though nothing had happened.

Imagine the negative impact those long periods of hurtful seething had on their relationship. Imagine how their unwillingness to repair the conflict quickly with apologies, forgiveness, and love must have chipped away at their closeness and trust.

As mentioned earlier, Dr. Gottman has found it takes five positive encounters between couples to counteract the impact of one negative encounter. When you allow an argument to simmer for days, without resolving the problem and reconnecting as a couple, you're compounding the conflict with multiple hurtful interactions.

Every cold stare, every moment of deafening silence, every missed attempt at reconciliation further entrenches the couple in a cycle of pain and divisiveness.

Not only does the couple have to engage in several positive interactions to make up for the *original* conflict, but now they've set themselves up for weeks of disconnection before they accumulate enough neutralizing, positive interactions to put them on sound footing again.

Of course, neither partner is motivated to initiate positive encounters when they are dealing with a backlog of resentment and pain. A small molehill of an argument has now grown into a big mountain of negativity, making it much more difficult to offer apologies, forgiveness, or compromise—much less to attempt positive, healing interactions.

The best thing you can do for the future health of your relationship is to address any initial conflicts, and the resulting emotional fallout, as quickly as possible. However, when both of you are angry, hurt, and confused *during* an argument, it's impossible in the moment to reconcile and reconnect.

It takes time and reflection to calm down and initiate a measured respectful resolution to patch up any hurt feelings. But it shouldn't take days. As tempting as it is to remain indignant, as justified as you might feel in your anger, as much as you believe it's your partner's turn to apologize first—don't allow these feelings to silence the better angels of your nature.

As soon as your anger has subsided, and your judgment has returned, reach out to your partner and initiate resolution and reconnection. Don't allow stubbornness or pettiness to prevent you from healing the rift as soon as possible. Even if you feel your partner is at fault and hasn't stepped up to apologize, you can still initiate repair to protect the intimacy, trust, and love you share together.

How to Develop This Habit

Healing hurts quickly is another variable habit that can be practiced only when you and your partner have an actual argument or disagreement.

You probably don't want to initiate conflict at the same time every day just so you can practice the habit of resolving the conflict quickly! That would certainly do more harm than good for your relationship.

But you can prepare in advance for the inevitable conflicts that arise down the road. This will help you know what to do to ensure you don't suffer longer than necessary.

Develop a time-out signal.

When a discussion devolves into a full-blown fight, you and your partner need a time-out from the escalating conflict in order to calm down and prevent further damage. The longer you interact while you are angry or hurt, the greater the chance you will drive a deeper wedge between you.

The moment you realize the conversation is going south, you need to initiate a break so you can come back together in a better frame of mind. The anger, irritation, or hurt feelings will need to be your triggers for initiating the time-out.

Talk with your partner about a signal or word you can use to indicate you both need a time-out. In the heat of the moment, you and your partner will want to continue defending your positions, so commit to one another now that you will honor this signal when one of you offers it during conflict.

Write down what the signal is, and consider posting a reminder in the rooms where you tend to have serious discussions or conflicts.

Separate and breathe.

During your time-out, go to separate rooms for fifteen to twenty minutes. Your first order of business is to simply calm down and regain emotional equilibrium.

Rather than stewing over the disagreement or preparing your defense, your job now is to simply breathe and relax. Sit down, close your eyes, and practice meditative breathing.

Breathe in slowly through your nose, and count on the out-breath, going from one to ten with each out-breath. Repeat this ten-count breathing exercise until you feel yourself getting calm and your anger dissipating.

If you find that fifteen to twenty minutes isn't enough time to manage your emotions, then wait a bit longer. Just don't let days go by before you get back together to work through the problem.

Reflect on your position and your partner's position.

Once you are calm and more centered, grab a pen and paper and write down all of your thoughts about your position related to the conflict and the corresponding feelings you experience. Write down everything you want your partner to understand about your side of the situation.

Once you have finished writing out your feelings and position, put yourself in your partner's shoes and write down what you believe his or her perspective is about the situation and how he or she might be feeling. Make a sincere effort to see the situation from your partner's point of view.

The last part of this exercise will allow you to be more empathetic to your partner and soften your heart so you can reconnect with kindness and compassion.

Initiate reconnection and resolution.

When you are both calm and have finished the reflection exercise, come back together to revisit the problem or conflict.

Begin by offering affection and words of love and affirmation. Give each other a hug. Hold hands. Say, "I love you," to one another. Do this even if you have some lingering resentment or frustration, as it will reinforce the positive and loving atmosphere you want for this conversation.

Take turns sharing your partner's perspective.

Begin the discussion by sharing what you believe your partner's feelings and position on the situation might be. Take turns doing this before either one of you responds.

Kicking off the conversation with empathy and understanding will make it easier to reach a compromise or resolution.

Present your own point of view and feelings.

Once you both have offered your thoughts on the other's perspective, you can each affirm or clarify your own thoughts and feelings and ask for what you need to help settle the issue.

You may need a behavior change from your partner, a compromise on a decision, or simple acknowledgment of your feelings. Try to be specific and direct (in a kind way) about what your goals are.

Be sure to use "I need" or "I feel" statements rather than blaming or shaming your partner. You will learn more about this in Habit #17.

Discuss and confirm a resolution.

Once you both have shared your points of view, your feelings, and what you hope to achieve, discuss any actions that you can agree on going forward.

Offer any behavior changes or compromises in the spirit of generosity and love rather than resentment or apathy.

After sharing and discussing the situation calmly, if you can't reach a resolution or one of you can't offer what the other needs, try not to get angry or frustrated. Sit on it for a few days to see if anything changes or if one of you has any new insights.

If not, consider talking with a therapist or other professional to help you reach a resolution.

Mindful Relationship Habit #14
Initiate Productive Conflict

One of the best ways to prevent a conflict from turning into a full-blown fight is by initiating productive conflict from the outset. We often initiate a conversation with our partner, knowing that the topic has the potential to start an argument. Yet we forge on anyway, arming ourselves to convince or coerce our partner into accepting our "rightness" about the situation.

Generally, this tactic backfires. Rather than mindfully working out a problem as a team, we end up seething in our separate corners, assured that the other person is unreasonable and selfish.

Empathy, negotiation, and compromise are essential to solving your solvable problems with your partner. As much as we might feel we have the right answer and want things to go our own way, we must put the health and strength of the relationship ahead of our own individual needs.

Initiating a conflict or potentially acrimonious discussion with some productive communication skills makes it a whole lot easier to navigate conflict with a lot less pain.

Unfortunately, research suggests that most of us are conflict averse, biting our tongue or actively taking steps to avoid conflict even when we long for a specific outcome. When we do engage, we may give in too quickly or compromise, failing to meet our own needs or devise useful solutions.

Or if we dig in our heels, trying to persuade our spouse that our belief is the right one, we miss the chance to learn more and to problem solve.

To improve communication as couples, we need to get better at initiating a productive conflict. What does that mean? It means understanding how to approach and resolve conflicts in ways that generate helpful solutions while protecting the relationship.

A productive conflict doesn't mean just being "nicer" about fighting. Rather, it means, having an intentional and healthy process for working through differences. And this is where negotiation becomes so important.

Negotiating well means using a process for creating better solutions—one that meets each partner's most important needs and preferences. There are specific negotiation habits that make up this process, and these habits will save you a lot of angst and frustration if you practice and learn them before the next conflict arises.

Remember, it's the way we handle conflict that matters—and avoiding conflict is extremely costly in the long run because we get worse outcomes and fail to seize opportunities to deepen our mutual understanding and intimacy.

These strategies can help you and your partner create the best conditions for coming up with good solutions while protecting the harmony of your relationship.

How to Develop This Habit

Again, this is a habit you can't practice until the next conflict situation arises. So you will need to be vigilant about remembering and practicing these steps when the situation calls for them.

That's why we believe it's valuable to set up a system for remembering the steps for a productive conflict and to write down that system so you commit to it.

One part of the system could be to post a reminder in a few places around your house so you remember to review and use the productive conflict skills we outline here. Of course, not all of your conflicts occur in your home, so putting a reminder on your phone that pops up every day can help you be prepared when a potential conflict arises.

If this is a habit you want to focus on for the next few weeks, put a rubber band on your wrist as a reminder to use these skills and agree to remind each other tactfully if necessary.

Before you begin the conversation, be sure to review the nine steps outlined here to keep you on track.

1. Choose the right time for a discussion.

We often decide to start up a serious conversation in the evening, when we're tired. After a long day of work or dealing with the kids, this can be the worst time to discuss a touchy topic.

Instead, schedule a time to bring up a potentially difficult conversation when you are both rested and in a good frame of mind. Be sure it's a time when you won't be interrupted or distracted.

2. Start with constructive language.

If you begin with something like, "I'd like to discuss the way you manage our money," it sounds like a criticism, as the problem appears to be with your partner.

Instead try something like, "I'd like to see if we can agree on some rules for our budget and money management." This is a more constructive way of opening the conversation by naming a positive goal rather than implying a problem with your partner.

3. Create mutual ground rules.

There are things you or your partner can say or do that will immediately get the conversation off to a bad start.

For example, using the words "always" and "never" can make your partner bristle. Talking early in the morning before you've had your coffee might not work for you. Starting a conversation with, "You do this" rather than "I need this," can put your partner on the defensive.

These are just some ideas, but you and your partner should come up with your own ground rules together.

4. Listen and validate first.

Remember that letting your partner feel heard and understood is a powerful way to help him or her feel safe and willing to be more generous and flexible in negotiation and compromise.

You don't have to agree with your partner to acknowledge what he or she is saying and feeling. Listening mindfully and attentively, nodding, and making affirmative noises or remarks can be enough.

Also, summarizing what you are hearing without judgment and asking your partner if you got it right is a powerfully constructive strategy.

5. Brainstorm several options.

When discussing a difficult or controversial topic, you may tend to rush quickly to a possible solution only to argue about whether the idea is good or bad.

Before you propose a solution, engage in a short period of brainstorming, where you both present several solutions without criticizing one another.

Once you have many possibilities on the table, you may find that combining several of them is easily agreeable to both of you.

6. Seek outside support from others.

Often we stew for days or weeks about things that are bothering us, only to let loose with a flood of criticisms that make healthy communication with your partner impossible.

Once you feel resentments brewing, find a confidant you can talk to about what is bothering you *before* you blow up, and ask them to help you.

A trusted friend or family member can help you clarify and articulate what is really bothering you and what your goals are. They can help you brainstorm a constructive way to open the conversation as well as think of questions to ask and ways to talk about your fears.

As new research on relationships has shown, this kind of support is highly effective in helping us better process information and create solutions.

7. Reframe criticism as complaint.

As relationship expert John Gottman has discovered, there is an important difference between a complaint and criticism. Complaint points to a behavior as the problem, where criticism implies a quality or trait of your partner is the problem.

However, if your partner opens with a criticism like, "You are so sloppy and disorganized," try not to wrangle about whether this is true. Instead, focus on specifics of the complaint and the behaviors your partner views as a problem.

Conversations that begin with criticism tend to degrade into defensiveness and counter-criticism; this makes reaching a solution all the more difficult.

Conversations that begin with a specific complaint, like, "I feel frustrated and overwhelmed when you forget to pick up your dirty clothes," tend to lead to more concrete solutions.

8. Use the phrase, "Is there anything else?"

At the beginning of the conversation, invite your partner to completely "empty their pockets" related to their issues with you.

For example, if your partner says, "I want to talk about your parents visiting for the holidays," instead of starting in with your thoughts, ask the question, "Is there anything else?"

There might be a deeper concern behind your partner's comment, like perhaps she feels left out when your parents visit. Allowing the real issue to emerge at the beginning of a discussion can save a lot of time and emotional energy.

9. Learn and practice repair moves.

Repair moves are words or actions that can lessen the tension if things begin to get heated in your conversation. Four powerful repair moves include:

1. Using lighthearted humor that you know will make your partner smile.
2. Reminiscing about a past happy or fun time together.
3. Apologizing for your part in creating a problem or causing your partner pain.
4. Using loving touch and affection.

These moves help defuse the tension so you can move on constructively with the conversation.

Mindful Relationship Habit #15
Develop Active Listening

One of the most valuable relationship habits you can develop is **active listening**. It's a skill that not only serves your partner and your relationship but also one that stretches you to become more loving, mindful, compassionate, and patient. It also leads to finding more effective solutions to *all* interpersonal problems.

This listening skill is important to use in situations when your partner is struggling with something and needs to find a solution, or when the two of you are working through a conflict. It is an essential habit to develop for the kind of productive conflict we outlined in Habit #14.

Active listening has tremendous therapeutic value in your relationship. It allows your partner a safe space to express his or her thoughts and feelings.

As your partner hears himself talk, he gains more clarity about his feelings or the problem at hand and becomes better equipped to find a resolution on his or her own or to work on one with you.

When your partner feels heard, an emotional burden is lifted, and he or she feels less stressed. As the listener, you don't have to agree with everything your partner says. You are listening to learn and to allow your partner to share and vocalize without judgment or anger.

Active listening is not an easy habit to master, mainly because most of us are more motivated to talk than listen. It's more challenging than basic listening because active listening requires you to be fully present. It is often needed during uncomfortable times when your partner is in pain or is angry or upset with you or the situation.

During the time you practice active listening, you aren't part of a "conversation" in the traditional sense. There's no give and take, sharing dialogue, or competing to talk. Rather, it's all about your partner and what he or she is trying to communicate—with words, with the words left unspoken, with body language, and with emotions.

It's natural to want to offer our partners a solution or advice and tell them what we think will make them happier, more successful, or ease their pain. This is usually done from a sincere desire to help them, but it can also become a knee-jerk reaction because, as a culture, we are encouraged to be solution-oriented. But patience, presence, and silence are the key ingredients for this powerful practice.

If you wish to be more of an active listener with your partner, you must be willing to do the following:

- » Allow your partner to dominate the conversation and determine the topic to be discussed.

- » Remain completely attentive to what he or she is saying.

- » Avoid interrupting, even when you have something important to add.

- » Ask open-ended questions that invite more from your partner (if he or she wants that).

- » Avoid coming to premature conclusions or offering solutions.

» Reflect back to your partner what you heard once he or she is done speaking.

How to Develop This Habit

Active listening is a habit that you can practice every day so that it becomes your go-to method of listening when it is required during difficult conversations.

Once you master the skills involved, you can practice active listening during any conversation. However, it might feel stilted and awkward to use it in day-to-day discourse when you're talking about what you did at work or how great the weather is.

That's why we suggest you practice active listening at a specific time of day, every day (or at least five consecutive days) for a few weeks, around a more serious or challenging topic that you have now or have experienced in the past.

Determine a time of day, trigger, and location.

Decide when you want to practice this habit and where you want to work on the skills. Choose a time when you are rested, in a good frame of mind, and less likely to be interrupted or distracted.

Since you'll be practicing this habit daily (or at least five days a week), determine a trigger to remind you to perform the habit. You might need a visual or phone reminder for the first week in addition to the trigger.

Also, select a calm, quiet place in your home to work on this habit for about twenty minutes.

Think about a topic for each practice session.

Come up with a personal challenge, need, goal, worry, hurt, or frustration you want to share with your partner during the practice session. These topics can be about your relationship with your partner, or they can relate to anything or anyone else in your life.

Since you'll be working on this habit for several weeks, you will need to come up with about twenty to thirty topics. Try to narrow down big issues into smaller discussion topics that take just a few minutes to discuss. You and your partner will take turns sharing your topic of discussion while the other person is the active listener.

Here are some topic ideas you might consider:

- » a small frustration with your partner you haven't vocalized
- » a worry about your child
- » a past pain related to your childhood
- » a fear or insecurity
- » a problem at work
- » an issue with a friend or family member
- » an unmet emotional need
- » a sexual need you haven't mentioned before
- » an upsetting situation that you witnessed
- » a dream or goal your partner doesn't know about
- » an area of confusion you are grappling with
- » a decision you need to make
- » a difference of opinion that is bothering you

» a financial concern

» a previous conflict that hasn't been settled

» an important memory or dream you want to share

» a realization or insight you've had

Remember, practicing this habit is more about learning to be an active listener rather than resolving a conflict or coming up with a solution. As a listener, you are giving your partner your full presence and acceptance, whether the topic is about you or someone else.

However, if a topic feels too intense for these practice sessions, you might want to save it for a time when you can focus on working out the problem.

As the speaker, share your topic or concern with your partner.

Decide who will be the first speaker during your practice sessions. As the speaker, share your topic by beginning with a statement like, "I'd like to talk about a worry I'm having about Jenny." Or, "There's something about our argument last week that I want to revisit."

If your topic relates to your partner and something he or she did that is bothering you, try not to point the finger of blame by using "you" statements, such as "You left the kitchen a mess again, and it's really bugging me. You are so thoughtless."

Rather, talk more about how you *feel* related to the situation and what you need. Help your partner understand not only the problem itself, but how the problem makes you feel and where those feelings are coming from. If there is something you need or want from your partner (or from someone else), state that need directly and clearly. In

Habit #17, we discuss how to communicate an issue with your partner more consciously.

After you have presented your topic, let your partner know it's okay to respond.

As the active listener, follow these steps:

1. Pay attention to body language.

Your entire demeanor needs to show that you are fully present. Turn off your phone so you aren't tempted to look at it. Try not to shift your eyes to look at your surroundings. Keep an open, accepting posture with your arms and legs uncrossed.

Lean in as your partner is speaking and look them in the eye on occasion (but not constantly). Try not to fidget or shift around to show impatience or irritation.

2. Reflect back to your partner.

When your partner is done speaking, repeat back to your partner what you heard him say about the topic, how she felt, and what he might need.

This helps your partner know that you were listening and allows you to confirm whether or not you heard everything he or she intended to communicate.

You can paraphrase, highlighting the most important points he or she shared. For example, you might say, "So what I heard you say was that you were upset this morning when you saw the dirty kitchen. It made you feel overwhelmed and like I didn't respect you enough to follow through on my commitment. Is that right?"

At this point, your partner may clarify something you missed or that wasn't communicated initially. For example, she might say, "Yes that's right, and I need you to be more consistent in following through on the chores that are yours."

If this happens, repeat back what your partner says until he or she confirms you understand everything clearly. You might say, "To feel more respected, you need me to be consistent with doing my chores."

3. Offer empathy, not sympathy.

Empathy is the grace note of active listening, as it allows your partner to feel safe, understood, and valued.

Sometimes we disguise empathic listening with words of sympathy. Perhaps we have experienced a similar situation, so we share it to let our partner know we understand. To your partner who is trying to process difficult emotions, it can feel like you're stealing their thunder or deflecting attention to yourself.

True empathic listening requires you to leave your stories and experiences at the door. You don't need to share them for your partner to know you understand what she is saying. Empathy says, "I get you," rather than "I get you because I've had it even worse."

4. Validate, but refrain from offering solutions.

As much as you might want to jump in and save the day with the perfect solution, don't do it. Just listen, nod, and make small comments that show you've heard what was said and that validate your partner's feelings.

But don't interrupt the process your partner is going through as he or she finds a way to express true feelings or needs.

You may find that if you wait, your partner will come to the same conclusion as you. If he or she asks you for a solution directly, don't offer it right away. Ask what he or she would suggest to you if the roles were reversed. Always try to give the power back to your partner during active listening.

5. Use open-ended, empathic, or dangling questions.

These invite deeper thought and consideration from the speaker. You might ask, "How did you feel about that?" Or "What do you think the best next step might be?"

You can also ask empathic questions that relate to your partner's emotional state. You might ask, "What were you feeling when that happened?" You might notice your spouse looks sad (or angry or fearful), and you can say, "You look sad. What's behind that?"

Try not to use leading questions with the intention of directing him or her to your solution. Your goal is to help your partner gain more clarity and self-awareness.

One way to do this is with a dangling question. This kind of question is an incomplete question like, "And if you had to do it again, you might ..." It leaves things hanging without an answer so your partner can determine the direction of the conversation.

6. Ask for more.

Your partner might offer a crumb of information, and you can tell it's just the tip of the iceberg. You know or suspect there's more just below the surface, and all he needs is a nudge to bring it forth. Even if you don't suspect there's more, there usually is, so it's always worth asking.

A question as simple as, "Is there more?" can unleash more of the story or the emotions behind the story. You can ask this several times (maybe slightly rephrased) until it's clear there is nothing more to add on the topic.

7. Repeat a phrase or word.

When your partner is sharing powerful or emotionally charged information, she may conclude with a sentence or statement that expresses her pain, worry, or frustration.

For example, if your partner discusses feelings of being betrayed by something private you shared, he or she might say, "I am so mad. I feel like I can't share secrets with you." You can repeat, "You are really upset, and it makes you hesitant to share with me." Or you can just say, "You're really mad about this."

This lets your partner know you are tracking with her rather than building a defense or response. It also gives her a cue to add more or clarify her statement.

When you repeat the word or phrase, try to imitate the same tone of voice your partner used. Don't repeat it as a question or with any judgment.

8. Allow for silences.

Long silences can be uncomfortable, but resist the urge to fill the silence with your suggestions or remarks. Allow your partner to use the silence to process his or her thoughts and then to break the silence when they are ready to speak.

When you give him this space without interrupting him, you are showing that you're there for him and willing to allow the time needed to gain clarity. When your partner realizes you aren't going to interrupt her, she is free to slow down and process more internally, which is necessary for analytical thinking.

You might find these silences and the slower-paced talking difficult to handle. But it is truly a gift just to be present and allow your partner the freedom to be reflective and to articulate at his or her own pace.

End the habit work by deciding on next steps.

When you have been the active listener and spent time allowing your partner to vent, he or she may come to some conclusion or solution themselves. Or maybe your partner may still be confused but feel greatly relieved and have more clarity around the problem.

It may be clear after you both take turns sharing a topic that you need to spend more time working on it together to reach a compromise or devise a solution.

Decide if you want to work on it immediately or wait until another time. Don't allow the problem or concern to linger for too long without addressing it. Be clear with one another about how you intend to deal with it now or later using some of the communication habits outlined in this book.

Mindful Relationship Habit #16
Practice Empathy

Have you ever had someone acknowledge and reflect back to you what you're feeling so perfectly that it made you tear up?

Has someone taken the time to sit with you quietly in your grief and just hold your hand?

Have you ever told someone your story, shared your pain, or acknowledged your shame, and they teared up in response to the powerful feelings you were expressing?

If so, these actions reflect the essence of empathy.

Empathy is one of the defining characteristics of emotional intelligence and is an essential skill to develop for a healthy, mindful love relationship.

Empathy calls for active listening, patience, intimacy, and selflessness. It requires a true desire to sit with your partner in his most difficult moments or share in her most joyous accomplishments.

To practice empathy, you must put yourself in your partner's shoes—to feel what he or she is feeling and to understand his or her perspective. You must be willing to step outside of your own needs in order to be fully engaged with this person you love more than anyone. Empathy also requires that you imagine how your partner is *impacted* by their emotions and to share in that impact.

Some people are naturally empathetic, but most of us need to learn or at least reinforce the skills of empathy. To do that, it's important to recognize its value, not only in our relationships, but also in our own personal growth.

Practicing empathy expands our understanding of ourselves and others. It connects us to the human condition—the suffering, the joys, the sorrows, and the longings we all share. It draws us closer to our partners and frees us to be vulnerable and authentic with them.

A successful love relationship requires a deep level of intimacy between two people. This closeness thrives on the empathic connection you have as a couple and the daily practice of empathy in all of your interactions.

Why is empathy so important in your relationship?

- » It helps you resolve conflict and misunderstandings, as you are more willing to see your partner's perspective and understand his or her feelings.

- » It gives you insight into the deepest recesses of your partner's emotional world, allowing you a fuller experience of the person you are sharing your life with.

- » It shows your partner that you love him or her enough to be fully engaged and present, bringing you closer to one another.

- » It strengthens your ability to be compassionate and nonjudgmental with other people in your life, not only your partner.

» It allows you to distance yourself from your own petty grievances, frustrations, and demands when you are focused on your partner and his or her needs and feelings.

As Daniel Goleman, author of *Emotional Intelligence: Why It Can Matter More Than IQ*, says:

> *Self-absorption in all its forms kills empathy, let alone compassion. When we focus on ourselves, our world contracts as our problems and preoccupations loom large. But when we focus on others, our world expands. Our own problems drift to the periphery of the mind and so seem smaller, and we increase our capacity for connection—or compassionate action.*

Empathy is a practice that will enrich your relationship and expand your experience of the world around you. By stepping outside of the cocoon of your own existence, problems, and emotions, you are connecting to a deeper, more mindful level of engagement and awareness.

If empathy doesn't come naturally to you, or if you've cut yourself off from empathy because you fear it will be too uncomfortable, you can learn to cultivate more empathy in your relationship with a little practice and effort.

How to Develop This Habit

Practicing the habit of active listening, as we outlined in Habit #15, is a great way to initiate the skills of empathy. As you learn to listen more mindfully to your partner with a compassionate and loving mind-set, you'll find that your ability to be empathetic expands to other interactions with your partner.

You'll also find that *you want to be* more empathetic with your partner because you recognize how powerful it is in deepening the intimacy between you.

Many opportunities to practice empathy will arise spontaneously in your regular interactions. So setting up a daily schedule to practice empathy isn't effective, as empathy must be authentic and relevant to real-life situations.

However, if this is a habit you want to strengthen, set up a reminder system to help you work on it. Notes posted in places where you will see them throughout the day, or a phone reminder that pops up at set times, can keep your commitment to this habit top of mind. You can also wear a rubber band on your wrist as another visual reminder.

Identify how your partner is feeling by paying attention.

One way to show empathy is by tuning in to how your partner is feeling without him or her having to tell you. Of course, you aren't a mind reader, but you can learn to read your partner's expressions, mood, and body language.

If this doesn't come naturally to you, it will take some practice. The best place to start is by simply paying more attention to your partner and what he or she seems to be projecting to you.

Are you seeing irritability, frustration, sadness, exhaustion? Have you noticed a subtle shift in her mood or a quietness that's settled over him?

Take the time to really notice your partner's demeanor, and if you sense something is off, ask him or her about it. "You seem a little tired. Is everything okay?" "I noticed you were reserved at dinner tonight. Is there something on your mind?"

By noticing and asking, you are communicating to your partner that you want to know more about his or her inner world. You are also inviting your partner to be with you, giving him or her a safe way to release pent-up emotions.

Mentally put yourself in your partner's shoes.

When your partner shares something with you that is causing pain, insecurity, discomfort, sadness, or any profound emotion, take a moment to think about how you would feel in the same situation; immerse yourself in those feelings for a moment.

If you would react differently in the situation, then put yourself in your partner's *emotional shoes* and reflect on how painful it is to experience the emotions your partner is experiencing. In most cases, it's not the situation itself that causes pain, but rather our reactions to the situation.

You may disagree with your partner's reaction, but that doesn't diminish his or her pain. Have empathy for the pain by sharing the suffering with him or her.

This exercise doesn't just apply to challenges or painful situations. You can also share in happy, positive, exciting experiences by emotionally merging yourself with your partner. Shared joy means increased joy for both of you. What a gift that is for your partner.

Verbalize that you are imagining how it would feel.

When you do the exercise of putting yourself in your partner's shoes, tell your partner that you are doing this. Say something like, "I'm thinking about how I would feel in this situation, and it would be awful. I know you are really suffering, and I am here with you."

If joy is doubled by sharing it, then pain is halved by sharing the burden of it with the one you love. When you verbalize that you "get" how your partner is feeling, it eases their pain, helping them to know they aren't alone. It also validates your partner's feelings, as you acknowledge the truth of their suffering.

Withhold judgment and show trust in your partner's wisdom/abilities.

Whether or not you agree with your partner's emotions, don't judge him or her for having them. Emotions are powerful, and when one is experiencing them, no amount of "common sense" or logical advice is helpful. Show empathy for your partner's powerful feelings by simply allowing him or her to express them.

It takes time and reflection to evaluate one's own emotions and to use calm judgment to assess an emotionally charged situation. Even then, your partner may or may not reach the same conclusion or opinion as you.

Show respect for your partner's personal judgment and inner wisdom by withholding your opinions unless specifically asked for them. When you are asked, try to get your partner to figure out the solution for himself or herself. By doing so, you will empower your partner and show your faith in him or her.

Take on some of your partner's responsibilities to better understand him or her.

High schools around the world are requiring teenage girls to carry around baby simulator dolls for a week that cry and wet themselves. The goal is to give teenagers a realistic view of parenthood in order to discourage teen pregnancy. Experiencing firsthand how demanding it is to be a parent is a highly effective form of birth control.

When you take on another person's day-to-day responsibilities, you have a much clearer perspective of what their life is like and can empathize with their unique challenges. It gives you much more clarity to *be* in someone's shoes rather than *imagining* yourself in them.

If you want to truly empathize with your partner, volunteer to take on their chores or obligations for a week (or at least a few days).

If your wife is the primary caretaker of the kids, invite her to go on a getaway for a long weekend so you can take over. If your husband pays the bills or handles yard work, then you volunteer to take on those responsibilities for a while.

Once you finish with this exercise, express to your partner how much better you understand what he or she deals with every day and how much you appreciate his or her efforts.

Consider your partner's needs in all decisions.

We all get stuck in our own heads, so focused on what we are doing that we neglect to include our partners. We might make ourselves a sandwich for lunch without asking if our partner wants one. Or we flip through TV channels looking for a show we like, not inquiring what our partner might enjoy watching.

Sometimes this lack of consideration can extend to bigger decisions or actions, like making a big purchase or accepting a job offer without including our partner. This can be extremely hurtful and disrespectful to your partner and destructive to your relationship.

Nearly every choice or decision you make will impact your partner in some way. The two of you are a team, and it's imperative that you consider your partner and his or her feelings and opinions in most of your actions and decisions, especially the big ones.

However, it's the small daily choices that really highlight your empathy and care for your partner. You ask your partner before changing the TV channel when you are both watching. You don't make the room colder or warmer before inquiring about your partner's comfort. You don't invite the new neighbors over for dinner without checking with your spouse to see if he or she is in the mood for guests.

Be present when needed.

One of the most important ways to show empathy is simply by being present for your partner—not only during times of challenge or pain, but also for the day-to-day decisions and minor issues that he or she experiences.

We get so distracted with our own problems or obligations that we aren't emotionally available for our partner. We have trouble pulling ourselves away from our computers or smartphones long enough to focus attention on what our partner is sharing with us.

As often as possible, shift your focus to your partner when he or she is in the room with you. Be fully present to what your partner is saying to you. Let your partner know in word and deed that he or she is your first priority most of the time; and when you are legitimately busy, tell your partner that you will be there for him or her shortly.

Practice a loving-kindness meditation.

The purpose of a loving-kindness meditation is to foster feelings of compassionate acceptance, kindness, and warmth toward other people. Who better to be the focus of this meditation than your love partner?

A variety of studies have proven the mental and physical benefits of practicing loving-kindness meditation, including one that found practicing seven weeks of loving-kindness meditation increased love, joy, contentment, gratitude, pride, hope, interest, amusement, and awe.

Your main goal in practicing this habit is to increase empathy and compassion toward your partner. The practice itself is quite simple.

Find a quiet place where you won't be interrupted. Sit in a chair or on a cushion on the floor with your legs crossed. Begin by counting your breaths for a few minutes as you would with any meditation to calm your mind.

Notice any areas of mental or emotional distress, self-judgment, or self-hatred. Begin the loving-kindness meditation by first showing compassion and love to yourself.

As you continue to breathe, speak out loud or to yourself the following phrases:

- » *"May I be free from inner and outer harm and danger."*
- » *"May I be safe and protected."*
- » *"May I be free of mental suffering or distress."*

> » *"May I be happy."*

> » *"May I be free of physical pain and suffering."*

> » *"May I be healthy and strong."*

> » *"May I be able to live in this world happily, peacefully, joyfully, with ease."*

After you speak these phrases about yourself, focus your attention on your spouse or partner, using his or her name:

> » *"May John be free from inner and outer harm and danger."*

> » *"May John be safe and protected."*

> » *"May John be free of mental suffering or distress."*

> » *"May John be happy."*

> » *"May John be free of physical pain and suffering."*

> » *"May John be healthy and strong."*

> » *"May John be able to live in this world happily, peacefully, joyfully, with ease."*

As you repeat each statement about your partner, be mindful of the meaning of each phrase and your deep desire for your partner's happiness. Focus on the feelings of love, tenderness, and compassion you have for your partner. Visualize your feelings of loving-kindness enveloping your partner with a warm, protective shield.

Modify your behavior out of empathy.

It is one thing to say you feel empathy and compassion for your partner. It's quite another to modify your own choices and behavior to *show* your empathy.

Let's say your partner was raised by an alcoholic parent. The memories of his or her experiences with this parent are painful and upsetting, so you choose not to drink around your partner because you don't want to trigger his or her pain.

Or your pregnant wife is feeling extreme morning sickness, and the smell of food cooking makes her nauseated. So you round up the kids early and take them to breakfast before school because you don't want your wife to suffer, even though it's inconvenient for you.

It does take energy and sacrifice to modify certain behaviors, but the effort you make speaks volumes about your love for your partner.

Mindful Relationship Habit #17
Use "I Feel" Instead of "You"

"You are so lazy. You never clean up after yourself."

"You never pay attention to what I say."

"You are self-centered, and you clearly don't care about my feelings."

Have you and your partner fallen into the habit of pointing the finger of blame or shame at one another when you feel wounded or angry? If you find yourself telling your partner what he is doing wrong or defining her by the behaviors that are bothering you, you're not alone. Most couples fall into this pattern after the initial infatuation phase begins to wane.

As a couple, you don't want to get stuck in this phase of deflecting blame and hurling criticism. In a mindful relationship, you need to focus less on criticizing your partner and more on communicating how the behavior makes you feel.

Dr. Harville Hendrix is the author of the *New York Times* bestselling book *Getting the Love You Want* and the founder of Imago Relationship Therapy. Hendrix sees a connection between the frustrations experienced in adult relationships and our early childhood experiences.

Through his work with thousands of couples, Dr. Hendrix has learned that when you understand each other's feelings and "childhood wounds" more empathically, you can begin to heal yourself and move toward a more conscious relationship.

He believes there are three stages in a committed relationship; when our relationship gets in trouble, we get stuck in the second stage and can't move on to the third.

The first stage is romantic love, which begins when you first fall in love with your partner. You feel a sense of oneness or completion that seems like it will last forever.

The second phase is the power struggle. During this phase, we begin to get more defensive, blame our partners, and focus more on protecting ourselves rather than engaging in the relationship. We start to dislike many of the things that made us fall in love in the first place.

Why does this happen? Because we are subconsciously looking for a partner who can make us more whole and complete—someone who will stimulate our growth. Our partners push our buttons and trigger some of our deepest wounds, usually from childhood. But if we work through these issues, we can achieve enormous personal growth.

Unfortunately, many couples get stuck in the power struggle phase and can't get off the cycle of defensiveness and repeat conflict.

For a relationship to reach its potential, couples need to become conscious of their power struggle and **begin the journey to the third stage of relationships called real or conscious love**. In a conscious relationship, you are willing to explore your own issues, so you feel safe enough to meet your partner's needs.

In a conscious relationship, you recognize your own unresolved childhood issues and how these issues are showing up in your current relationship. When you find fault with your partner, you can shine a light on your own dark experiences to see how you are projecting your baggage onto your partner.

Just taking a moment each time you have a frustration to consider where this upset is coming from can do wonders for easing the conflict in your marriage.

Also, as you work toward a conscious relationship, you begin to let go of illusions about your partner and see him or her not as your savior but as another wounded person like you who is struggling to be healed and to grow.

You also begin to take responsibility for communicating your needs to your partner without expecting him or her to instinctively know them. You become more intentional in your communication so that you keep the channels of mutual understanding open.

Through this process, you learn how to value one another's needs and wishes as much as you value your own—because this contributes to the health of the relationship and your own happiness.

One way to encourage a more conscious relationship is by changing a few simple words in your communication with one another and being more intentional in expressing your frustrations and hurt feelings without divisive criticism or defensiveness.

When you express how you feel and what triggered your feelings, rather than blaming your partner, you change the entire dynamic of your conflict from divisive to collaborative.

How to Develop This Habit

It's useful to practice this habit before a real conflict arises that requires the skills involved. You can do this in a role-play situation that doesn't feel too awkward or stilted.

Consider working on it a few times a week for about ten to fifteen minutes so you get the hang of the language involved. As with all your habit work, find a suitable time and trigger to help you remember to work on it.

You and your partner will take turns sharing a complaint or concern with one another, focusing on your own feelings and personal history rather than on your partner's perceived flaws.

Focus on your feelings.

In preparation for your habit work, think about an issue with your partner in which you might want to criticize your partner's behaviors or decisions. This could be something he or she said or did recently that is bothering you or making you feel wounded.

However, rather than dwelling on your partner's shortcomings, think about what his or her behavior triggered in you.

Was it anger? Embarrassment? Disrespect? Feeling unloved?

Anger is often a surface emotion, covering up a deeper insecurity or wound triggered by your partner's words or actions. There may be more than one emotion that was triggered, so dig deep to consider the layers of feelings that might be involved.

Consider related past wounds.

As Dr. Hendrix reminds us, many of our triggered feelings relate to childhood wounds or past negative experiences. Your wife's nagging may remind you of your harsh and critical mother. Your husband's aloofness may trigger your pain related to a cold and emotionally unavailable father.

When your partner better understands how his or her behavior triggers these old wounds and how it makes you feel, he or she will have more empathy and motivation to change the behavior.

Not all frustrations are related to your childhood or past experiences, but many are. When you isolate these situations, you have a real opportunity for healing and growth, especially with a compassionate partner.

Use an "I feel" statement.

If you are sharing an issue, focus on your own feelings in a succinct way without too many words.

Start with the words, "When you," to describe the bothersome behavior, followed by the words, "I feel," to describe your feelings, rather than assigning blame to your partner.

For example, you might say, "When you talk down to me, I feel shamed and disrespected," rather than, "You are such a know-it-all. Stop telling me what to do!"

If you need some inspiration for feelings words, use this list of emotions on Barrie's blog to help you.

Use "It reminds me of" to communicate past wounds.

After you communicate the issue and how it makes you feel, share the childhood or past wound that your partner's behavior has triggered for you (if this applies). Try to share a specific example rather than a general issue.

For example, you might say:

"When you talk down to me, I feel shamed and disrespected. It reminds me of the times when my dad would criticize me and call me stupid for not making straight A's."

Ask for the support you need.

If your partner said to you out of the blue, "Can you please help me heal from a painful experience in my past?" you would likely say, "Of course, I am here for you. What can I do?"

When your partner expresses that *your behavior* has triggered pain, he or she is also reaching out for your help, even though it may not seem like it. Of course, it's hard to offer that help when your partner strikes back with wounding, critical words.

That's why it's important for the partner who is sharing the problem to ask directly for what he or she needs in order to facilitate healing and reconnection.

After you communicate the issue, how it made you feel, and the past wound it triggered, tell your partner directly how he or she can help you.

"I need you to speak more respectfully and kindly to me. This will bring me closer to you and help me feel safe that you won't treat me like my dad did. Will you do that?"

Practice in writing first.

It might help to first write out your thoughts about the issue you will communicate to your spouse during your practice sessions using the following template:

When my partner _____,

Then I feel _____.

It reminds me of _____.

I need my partner to _____.

Add active listening to your practice.

Once you both get the hang of communicating your complaints or hurts using the language outlined here, add active listening as part of the dialogue practice, as explained in Habit #15.

This will give you the opportunity to practice a conscious dialogue in which one partner presents an issue using conscious language and the other listens empathically.

Remember:

» Use "I" words when describing your feelings as the speaker.

» Describe what past pain the issue triggered for you (if any).

» The listener should validate the partner with words like, "That makes sense," or "I can see that."

» The listener should mirror the partner's words, then ask, "Is that right?"

» The listener should ask, "Is there more?" to give the speaker the chance to say everything needed.

» The listener should empathize with the partner's feelings with "I imagine you must feel …"

» The speaker should ask for what he or she needs to help resolve or heal the situation.

These practice sessions are to help you learn how to communicate more mindfully and empathically, but you may not be able to completely resolve your issue during these sessions.

You may need to revisit Habit #14 for ideas on resolving issues and reaching compromise once you have had a conscious dialogue about a problem or area of conflict.

Mindful Relationship Habit #18
Drop the Buts

Consider how it feels when someone tries to apologize to you and includes the word "but." "I'm sorry I forgot our lunch date, but I got distracted with work." "I'm sorry I hurt your feelings, but you shouldn't have asked my opinion." The "but" makes it feel like a half-baked concession attached to a poor excuse or qualifier.

In a conversation with your partner, using the word "but" has the same nullifying effect. It tends to brush aside what your partner has just said; it often minimizes what they're saying.

For example, your partner says, "I really want to go on that trip to New York with our friends." If you say, "That sounds fun, but we really shouldn't spend that money right now," you have essentially said, "I discount your idea and your feelings. I know best."

Even when you acknowledge your partner's feelings or ideas, if you attach a "but" to the back end of your acknowledgment, your partner will feel slighted. All he or she will hear is your contradiction or differing opinion.

You can certainly disagree with your partner without shutting him or her down out of the gate. In fact, if you listen open-mindedly without immediately expressing your opinion, you might learn something you haven't previously considered. You might find a way to a compromise or discover a better solution.

But you can't do that with a big but in the way. Endeavor to stop using this communication-quashing word when responding to your partner. Instead, try using connecting words and phrases like, "I understand what you are saying, and another thought is," or "That's a good idea. Also we could consider …" In this way, you validate your partner and offer another suggestion for you both to consider.

You can also use the word "and" instead of "but" to make your point without diminishing your partner's statement. For example, "I like the idea of going on the trip to New York, and I'd like us to go over our finances to see if we can swing it." This statement sounds more positive and encouraging while still addressing the concern about the expense.

Once you begin working on this habit, you'll discover how often you use the word "but" in conversation with your partner. Of course, there are some situations when it is necessary in order to explain a valid caveat (i.e., "I want to meet you for lunch today sweetie, but I have an important client call at 12:30."). However, you need to be mindful about using it to contradict or undermine your partner's opinion, idea, or position.

How to Develop This Habit

This habit involves dropping a negative behavior and replacing it with a more positive one. Instead of using the word "but" to qualify or minimize your partner's statement by redirecting to your own opinion, you should replace it with the word "and" or phrases like,

> » "I understand what you are saying, and another thought is …"

> » "That's a good idea. We could also consider …"

> » "That makes a lot of sense. Let's talk about how to …"

> » "Tell me more about your idea and how we can do this."

You will need to practice this habit spontaneously, when the situation arises that calls for you to drop and replace the bad habit.

Begin by noticing your "buts."

The best way to drop this bad habit is simply by noticing how often and when you say it. Use a visual reminder, like a rubber band on your wrist, to help you stay aware of the word slipping out in conversation with your partner.

You and your partner can also make a game of it and remind one another when you notice the other person using the word. This reminder should be playful and gentle—not accusatory or shaming. The goal is to help one another change the behavior in a loving way that helps both of you.

Analyze and rephrase your reply.

As mentioned before, some "buts" are necessary and useful. Others are diminishing and hurtful. When you become aware of using this word, analyze your statement to see if you need to rephrase it to be more positive and affirming.

Take a look at these examples:

"I love the idea of planting a garden with you, and I want to do it, but until my back is better I can't." (This is an acceptable "but," as the speaker is simply relaying a fact that makes the idea presented unworkable for now.)

"Planting a garden sounds great, but it's a lot of work, and I already have a lot on my plate." (This is a bad "but," as the speaker immediately quashes the idea with general negative statements.)

Another way to phrase this statement could be, "Planting a garden sounds great, and I think it would be fun to do together. Let's look at how much time we think it will take and how we can work it into our schedules."

Every time you catch yourself using the word, stop and examine whether or not it needs to be rephrased. If so, restate your reply to your spouse or partner in a more mindful way.

Affirm and respond positively in general.

Have you noticed how easy it is to immediately jump to a negative response when your partner presents something you don't agree with?

We quickly counter with why the idea is bad or won't work or why our point of view is better or more "right."

All of us do this from time to time, and it causes tiny paper cuts of pain for our partners to be shut down so quickly. Perhaps with some additional thought or consideration or more information, we might discover our partner's ideas have more validity than we initially thought. Perhaps we haven't heard everything we need to hear in order to respond.

A great way to prevent the "buts" from showing up in your responses is by simply delaying your response. Ask your partner to tell you more instead. Explore the idea or information further with him or her. Give your partner the courtesy of considering an idea for more than a nanosecond, and affirm that you have fully heard what he or she has said.

If there are legitimate concerns about why something is wrong or won't work, your partner will likely reach that conclusion at some point on his or her own.

Mindful Relationship Habit #19
Learn to Be Mindfully Direct

Are you and your partner able to be direct with one another, communicating your desires and needs without anxiety, insecurity, or discomfort? Or do you find yourself holding back or using more passive ways of communicating your needs?

Because no one really enjoys conflict or discomfort, we sometimes skirt around issues, vaguely suggesting what we want without saying exactly what we mean. Some of us confuse being direct with being rude or demanding, so we're reticent to speak up for fear of offending. Or there are those who fear rejection or put-downs from their partner if they speak up directly and share their thoughts and feelings.

If a topic is embarrassing or emotionally charged, we can hold back from the desire to avoid uncomfortable, awkward confrontations. And then there are the times we think our partner should read our minds and just intuit what we want without us having to tell them. We associate love with mind reading, which is a setup for resentment and unhappiness.

Some people have a more difficult time putting their feelings into words or articulating exactly what they want because they haven't taken the time to self-reflect and understand their own needs and emotions.

Being evolved adults (and a healthy couple) calls for both partners to say what they feel, ask for what they need, and express themselves openly—with confidence and kindness. It also calls for both partners to respond to direct communication without defensiveness, blaming, criticism, or anger.

When you speak directly to your partner, your language is clear, straightforward, and unambiguous. There is no pretense or hidden message in direct communication; its purpose is quite simply to get or give information and open a dialogue with your partner. It involves the two-way, free-flowing sharing of thoughts, feelings, and ideas in a way that leads to solutions.

You would think this would be easy, and for some it is. But most of us have a hard time communicating directly in some areas of our relationship, so we resort to all sorts of verbal gymnastics in order to express ourselves. Or we bottle up our feelings until they overflow and spill out in unproductive ways.

Let's look at some of the ways you might not be communicating directly in your relationship and what you can do about it.

You hint, wish, and hope without saying what you mean.

Let's say you've had an especially hard day, and you're starting to come down with a cold. It's your turn to prepare dinner, but you really don't feel like it. So you say to your partner, "Boy, I feel like a truck hit me, but I guess I need to start fixing dinner."

What you really mean is, "Honey, I am not feeling well. Would you please fix dinner tonight, and I'll pick up the slack next week?"

With the first statement, you hint at the problem but never directly ask for a solution. Leaving vague clues about what you want is passive and doesn't always result in your partner catching on to your meaning. Save yourself and your partner time and emotional energy by cutting to the chase in the first place and stating plainly what you need.

You might also find yourself hoping and wishing for something from your partner without articulating it. You hope he will see how much you need a hug. You wish she would initiate sex more often. But from discomfort or the false belief your partner should be a mind reader, your feelings go unvoiced.

If you just wish and hope for what you want without saying it, the odds are slim that your needs will be considered. You have to take personal responsibility for stating what you need in a way that is thoughtful but clear to your partner.

You wonder, guess, and assume without asking.

Some of the worst conflicts in relationships are the result of speculating and then reacting to your own assumptions. You notice your spouse has gotten quiet, and you conclude he's mad at you. You assume your partner doesn't want to go to the movies with you, but you neglect to ask her. You wonder why your boyfriend doesn't like holding hands in public, so you assume he's losing interest in you.

When you speculate like this, you feel powerless and confused. You also set the stage for misunderstandings and arguments. Have you ever said something to your partner like, "You seemed mad at me, so I assumed you didn't want to go out," only to have your partner say, "What are you talking about? I never said I was mad. I really wanted to go out."

We often create stories in our heads about what our partner is thinking or feeling, or what his or her intentions might be. Even with someone we know so well, we don't *always* know what they mean or how they'll respond.

If you want clarity and peace of mind, ask. Don't just assume, guess, and wonder. Asking also shows that you respect your partner enough to confirm what's on their mind and in their heart.

Try to use open-ended questions that invite full disclosure rather than yes or no questions based on your guess or assumption. So rather than saying, "Are you mad at me for some reason?" you might say, "How are you feeling about our connection right now?" Instead of saying, "I guess you don't want to go to the movies tonight," you would say, "What do you feel like doing tonight?"

Another way of being indirect in your communication is stating what you don't want rather than what you would like.

Framing a statement to your partner with the negative phrase, "I don't want," is putting him or her on the defensive before you finish uttering the sentence. It leads with negativity rather than clarity.

Think about the difference in these two sentences and how you'd react to them:

» "I don't want your parents to come over on Sunday."

» "I would like to spend Sunday taking a hike together and having brunch."

The second statement invites a more positive response and gives more information to your partner. It also promotes the opportunity for a dialogue rather than throwing up a roadblock.

Being direct with your partner might feel uncomfortable in some situations. If you are someone who is more reticent to speak up, it can take some time to develop this habit.

But speaking up in a way that is confident, clear, and kind shows your partner that you respect yourself and that you value your relationship enough to say what you mean.

Holding back and being vague might feel safer in the short term, but it doesn't serve the long-term goals of healthy communication and honesty in your relationship.

How to Develop This Habit

You can practice the habit of being more direct in your communication by practicing dialogues in which you and your partner share in asking for something that you want or need from the other.

Set aside a time at the beginning of the week to have the dialogue for sharing your need. These dialogues will feel stilted and unnatural at first, but with practice, you will be able to use a more conversational style that suits you as a couple.

The purpose of each phrase in the dialogue "script" is to keep you on track so the conversation doesn't devolve. Sticking to the script will allow you to listen more empathically to one another and reach a resolution more quickly.

In what ways have you been indirect or holding back?

Consider some unmet needs or requests you have for your partner that you haven't expressed out of anxiety or discomfort. These might be topics you've tried to express passively or indirectly, but your partner hasn't gotten the message.

Make a list of anything that comes to mind. Some ideas might include:

- » needing more physical affection
- » desiring something different in your sex life
- » wanting to spend less time with in-laws
- » needing more time and attention from your partner
- » wanting your partner to do something with you that he or she may not enjoy
- » needing your partner to handle a task or chore
- » needing your partner to participate more in parenting
- » wanting to buy something but fearing resistance from your partner
- » wanting your partner to join you for counseling
- » needing your partner to be healthier or lose weight
- » needing more time for yourself
- » wanting to quit your job or change jobs

Choose the least challenging topic to begin your practice.

If you have trouble being direct, you may not want to start this habit practice with the topic that makes you the most uncomfortable. Get your feet wet with a topic you can discuss without too much anxiety.

As you build your confidence speaking directly, you can address more challenging topics.

As the listener, allow your partner to be direct without reacting.

One reason people aren't direct is because they fear how their partner will react. It's hard to be forthright when you worry your partner will be angry, defensive, or wounded.

As you practice making direct statements and requests, you both need to listen without offense or anger when your partner makes his or her statement. It can be hard to hear something that reflects on a weakness or that triggers a fear or insecurity, but you must learn to hear your partner's needs without showing negative reactions.

Remember, it's also hard for your partner to be direct with you, so don't make it harder by reacting badly. You will have time during the dialogue to present your feelings and reactions mindfully after you have listened to your partner.

Hopefully through this habit practice, both you and your partner will learn how to present your needs directly but also with kindness and empathy.

Ask for what you want, not what you don't want.

Remember, you have a need or desire, so state what that is in positive words, rather than telling your partner what he or she needs to stop doing or to change.

State your need or desire succinctly, directly, and thoughtfully using "I" statements. It is easier just to get the words out without any buildup, qualifiers, or hemming and hawing.

> » "I want us to work out together so we can both lose weight."

> » "I need your presence at my family reunion."

> » "I'd like for us to go to marriage counseling together."

> » "I need your help getting dinner on the table tonight."

As the listener, reflect, confirm, and ask for more.

When your partner makes a direct statement about a need, mirror the statement and confirm you heard it correctly.

"You need me to join you for the family reunion. Is that correct?"

If you heard your partner correctly, ask your partner if he or she has more to share by saying, "Is there more?"

As the speaker, offer more details or specific information.

This is the time to say something like:

> » "Yes, I need you at the reunion because I need your support, and I don't want to be the only person there without a spouse."

Or

> » "I want us to go to counseling to work on our issue about your mom so we don't keep arguing about it."

As the listener, confirm again and reply.

Once again, mirror back what you heard your partner request, asking if you heard it correctly. Then validate that you understand why this request is important to your partner. "I can see how much you need me at the reunion and why it would make you uncomfortable if I'm not there."

Respond back to your partner with what you are willing to do to honor the request. You may need to work on a compromise if the request is something that is hard for you or something you don't want to do. "I can go to the gym twice a week, but three times is hard with my work schedule. Does that work?"

You may also need more information about the request if you don't understand why it's being made. For example, if your partner wants to go to marriage counseling, you might say, "Can you tell me more about why you want to go to counseling?"

What if I can't honor the request?

Do your best to honor a request or reach a compromise if it's clear it's important to your partner, even if it's not important to you. However, there may be requests you simply can't honor or compromise on right now. You may need more time to think about the request or gather more information.

If this is the case, explain your position with empathy and love:

"I know how important it is that I go to the reunion with you. I really want to be there for you because I love you and want to support you. Right now, I'm still reeling from the blowup at the last family gathering, and I don't think I can be with everyone again so soon."

"I understand why you want a new car and how long you've been driving this clunker. I want you to have a new car too. We are so stretched financially right now that I just can't agree with this purchase until we can afford it."

"I see how I haven't been available for you in the last few weeks, and I know it makes you feel like I don't care. Until tax season is over, I don't see how my schedule can change. I hope you can be patient with me for a bit longer."

If your direct request can't be honored right away, you can always revisit the issue later on, as time has a way of changing our minds and our circumstances. Until then, try to respect your partner's response and focus your attention on all of the other things he or she does for you.

Mindful Relationship Habit #20
Manage Your Anger Constructively

How many of your conversations with your partner have led to one or both of you becoming angry. There are few other people in our lives who have the ability to push our buttons and rile us up like our partners can. But expressing your anger in hurtful, self-indulgent ways wreaks havoc on your relationship and your health.

Too often we say and do things in anger we later regret, things that make us look petty and cause a deep rift in our connection with our partner. Regular episodes of anger can erode your partner's love, trust, and goodwill. Over time, it can make your partner fearful of giving and receiving love and can damage his or her self-esteem.

But it's not just your relationship that suffers. Conflict and anger in marriage are linked to physical problems including increased blood pressure, impaired immune function, and a poorer prognosis for spouses with coronary artery disease and congestive heart failure.

A 2009 study underscores that anger from one spouse is a contributing factor to depressive illness in the other spouse. "The more hostile and anti-social behavior exhibited, the more depressed the spouses were after three years."

Parents' anger toward one another can also be very damaging to children. It is upsetting to them, and young children often believe they are the cause of the anger, piling guilt feelings on top of their fear.

Although expressing your anger aggressively can temporarily make you feel better, it isn't a mindful strategy for strengthening your relationship. In most cases, showing anger makes it much harder to reach a resolution. And in spite of claims to the contrary, research has proven that venting your anger only makes you angrier.

As a result, you often have to spend more time dealing with the fallout from your angry behaviors than you do in dealing with the real issue at hand. It can take weeks or months to heal from the pain of cruel words or to rebuild trust after an angry outburst.

Unfortunately, you can't just stop yourself from feeling anger. Something your partner says or does or neglects to do can trigger a cascade of furious feelings. You can no more to block these feelings than you can stop a steaming locomotive racing down the tracks.

As corrosive as it can be, anger does serve a purpose in revealing the seriousness of the issue you and your partner are facing. Your anger may reveal a backlog of feelings from the past that have been simmering beneath the surface and need sorting out. Anger can energize you to respond and take action.

Anger can also lead to productive dialogue when you learn how to express it in ways that don't emotionally scar your partner and sabotage your relationship. In a mindful, conscious relationship, you don't indulge in outbursts or tirades. You choose to control your anger and express it appropriately.

You've likely learned the hard way that responding to your partner while angry isn't productive. The best thing anger can do for you during conflict with your partner is serve as a big flashing stop sign. Once you realize you are angry, use whatever remains of your rational mind to take a few deep breaths, count to ten, and excuse yourself from the conversation.

Of course, you need the ability to recognize when you are becoming angry before you can act on it. Awareness is the first step in managing your feelings. Some of us repress our angry feelings until they surprise us by bursting forth in a tantrum. Sometimes anger is mild or moderate, making it harder to recognize, but it can still cause an undercurrent of discord between you and your partner.

Either way, there are definite signs and bodily changes that accompany the temperature rise in your feelings that can make you more aware of what's happening. Paying attention to these changes can help you manage your anger before it gets the best of you.

Here are some signs that you are beginning to feel angry:

» Adrenaline and other chemicals begin to surge through your body.

» Your heart rate speeds up, which prepares you for aggressive action.

» Your face flushes and your hands get sweaty.

» You may point a finger to emphasize your words or form a clenched fist to appear threatening.

» You either clench your jaw to contain your angry feelings, or you start spouting harsh and critical words.

» Your voice becomes increasingly loud and fast.

» You cross your arms in a defensive posture, and you begin to feel defensive.

» You become more focused on your partner's perceived bad behavior and lose the capacity to see your part of the problem.

» You don't want to hear anything that contradicts your angry beliefs. You are hyper focused on yourself.

» The executive functioning part of your brain, allowing you to analyze and solve problems, appears to shut down. You are in fight-or-flight mode, putting you at risk for aggression.

The angrier you become, the more negatively you perceive the situation, as your senses are giving you unreliable data. You overgeneralize and see your partner as worse than he or she really is.

Recognizing this unruly emotion before it erupts and managing it appropriately can mean the difference between reaching a calm resolution or seething in separate corners and nursing your wounds. You may not be able to control anger from bubbling up, but you can prevent it from spilling over in destructive ways by learning new habits to deal with your feelings.

How to Develop This Habit

Managing your anger is a habit you will need to work on in real life situations in order to master it. This makes it a much harder habit to develop, as you not only have to remember to put the habit into practice in real time, but you must do so while experiencing a flood of powerful emotions.

One way to overcome this roadblock is by embracing how necessary and valuable this habit is to the long-term health and happiness of your relationship.

Ongoing anger by one or both partners will erode your intimacy and eventually spell the end of your relationship. Even occasional outbursts of anger will set you back in your closeness and require a lot of time and effort to repair the rifts.

If one or both of you has a problem managing angry feelings and expressing them productively, this is a habit you should prioritize. Make a conscious decision as a couple to protect your closeness by learning new skills for communicating without angry words.

Here's how to do this:

Recognize how anger appears for you and what triggers it.

Revisit the list of physical and emotional symptoms of anger outlined earlier. How does anger typically show up for you first? Do you notice a small irritation? Do you have physical symptoms? Do you cross your arms? Do you feel like crying?

Also think about the situations, words, or conflicts that have triggered your anger in the past. Do you see any patterns here? Maybe there is one main issue or past pain that is still raw. There could be an area where you feel insecure or unappreciated.

Knowing what triggers you and how your anger begins to creep in can help you recognize what's happening before it gets out of control.

Notice passive-aggressive anger.

Some people don't feel safe or comfortable expressing anger openly, in either constructive or aggressive ways. Instead, they revert to passive-aggressive behaviors to make their feelings known.

Passive-aggressive behavior can manifest in many ways but has the common feature of nonverbal negativity, resistance, and confusion. It can show up as procrastination, learned helplessness, stubbornness, resentment, sullenness, or purposeful failure to handle requested tasks.

In relationships, one partner might passively punish the other by withholding affection or sex, being chronically late, creating drama, sabotaging, or playing the guilt card.

Using passive anger can be as destructive to your relationship as overt aggression. It is an insidious way of confusing and undermining your partner without open and authentic communication. It has no place in a mindful relationship.

If you notice any of these behaviors cropping up in yourself, recognize that they are signs of anger that should be addressed. These behaviors can poison your relationship.

Cut back on alcohol.

When you are inebriated or have had just a few drinks, your judgment is impaired, and you have fewer filters between your brain and your mouth. Alcohol reduces your inhibitions, so you feel freer to mouth off or say inappropriate things.

Alcohol also compromises your ability to properly evaluate the intentions of people around you. Innocent words or actions are misconstrued because your perspective changes, and you lose the faculty of reasoning.

The more you drink, the worse it gets. In fact, scientists have linked aggression to drinking too much alcohol. For those who are already prone to anger, adding alcohol to the mix is like adding fuel to a fire.

Remind yourself and your partner to avoid any serious conversations or hot-button topics when you are drinking. Even one drink can impair you enough to impact your ability to control your anger.

Consider other risk factors for irritability and anger.

In addition to alcohol consumption, there are other reasons you may be more prone to feeling angry.

Possible risk factors for anger include being tired, hungry, over-whelmed, premenstrual, stressed out, feeling out of control, or being sick. Anger is cumulative, so maybe something happened earlier to trigger your anger more easily.

Being aware of these risk factors can help you avoid or postpone discussions that might go south quickly.

Use angry feelings as a stop sign.

You can prevent your angry feelings from doing harm to your relationship when you catch them early. The moment you notice yourself feeling irritated or agitated, use the stop sign imagery to literally stop, look, and listen, as you would do in your car with a real stop sign.

Pause the conversation and remove yourself from the situation (but don't storm off in anger). Tell your partner in a reasonable tone that you need a break to calm down then step out of the room. Take some slow, deep breaths, focusing on your breathing rather than your angry thoughts.

Drink some cold water to cool yourself down. Do something distracting like folding laundry or cleaning out your car. Take enough time to allow your anger to dissipate so that you can think more clearly.

> **Note:** If your partner wants to step away to calm down, don't try to force him or her to continue the conversation. You may want an immediate resolution, but you will save yourself a lot of time, energy, and angst by waiting until you are both calm to resume.

Analyze the situation calmly.

Once you've calmed down, you need to look at yourself and the situation through rational eyes. You might want to take notes as you review the situation and your reactions to it; that way, you can refer to the notes when you talk to your partner.

Consider any possible miscommunications or misunderstandings that might have led to your irritated feelings. Did your partner mean to offend you? Could you have misinterpreted his or her tone? Was some information left out?

Ask yourself what role you played in the difficulty. For a moment, take the focus off of your partner and look at yourself.

» Could your anger be coming from something else and be misdirected at your partner?

» Did the situation trigger a deeper pain or past memory that is showing up as anger?

» Are you jumping to conclusions or allowing your ego to get in the way?

» Do you have a sense of entitlement about your position that is making you feel angry?

Believe it or not, if you discover you played a larger role in the upset, you will feel calmer.

Examine the deeper emotions under your anger.

Being able to articulate the feelings beneath your anger will help you and your partner better understand why you were triggered and what the real issue is.

Was your anger a cover for insecurity, feeling unloved, embarrassment, shame, guilt, or some other deeper emotion? If you remove the hard veneer of anger, what is left underneath? Being vulnerable about these feelings can lead to a speedier healing between you and your partner.

What is your goal?

Determine what your ultimate goal is in regard to the situation and what made you angry. Rather than focusing on what your partner did wrong (if that's the source of your anger), focus on what you want.

For example, instead of saying, "You promised to clean the garage this weekend, and you never follow through," say, "I need to feel confident that you will keep your word when you commit to something." This opens the door to finding solutions without casting blame.

Brainstorm solutions you can bring to the table when you reconnect with your partner. Be sure to think about solutions that you yourself can take rather than just focusing on what your partner needs to do.

What do you need to improve or change to lessen the tension, reach a compromise, or solve the problem?

Reconnect and listen.

Don't wait days to reconnect. As soon as you both feel calmer, resolve things as quickly as possible. After you've looked at the situation with a clear head, it's time to go back and listen to your partner's perspective.

Reconnect with your partner with the goal of simply hearing his or her side of the issue. You will need to employ empathic listening skills, as outlined in Habit #15, at the outset of the conversation.

For now, just remember to focus on your partner's words without preparing your defense or offense. Listen to learn and better understand. Hearing your partner's point of view without dealing with angry feelings can be surprisingly liberating and healing for you. Then you will have a turn to share your feelings and the observations you made while apart.

You can both practice active listening skills with each other so that you feel understood and validated before you reach a resolution or compromise.

Express legitimate anger constructively.

If your partner has said or done something that causes justifiable anger, it is acceptable and necessary for you to express how you feel. However, you can show your anger and talk about your feelings without aggression.

You can be direct without wounding. You can show frustration, hurt feelings, disappointment, or disbelief without getting even or blowing up.

Try not to use judgment statements or blame, even if feel your partner was being selfish or thoughtless. Focusing on your own feelings gives your partner room to self-reflect without getting defensive. It opens his or her heart to the suffering the behavior has caused you. Remember the habit of using "I" statements rather than "You" statements when expressing your anger.

Like:

>> "When you forgot my birthday, I felt hurt and unloved, like I'm a low priority."

>> "I feel lonely and abandoned when you spend every weekend golfing with the guys."

>> "When you give me instructions on how to drive, it makes me feel inadequate, like you don't trust my abilities."

When you share your feelings rather than pointing a finger of blame, your partner will be more receptive to making a behavior change. Just be sure you ask for the change respectfully.

Like:

>> "Birthdays are really important to me. Would you please set up a reminder system so you don't forget again?"

>> "I have a request. Would you please limit your golf outings to one weekend a month? I want us to spend more time together as a couple."

» "When we are in the car together, would you please refrain from giving instructions if I'm driving?"

By taking the time to manage your anger and express it constructively, you're not only saving yourself from future regret and difficulties in your relationship—you're also training yourself to be the mindful and evolved partner and person you want to be.

Mindful Relationship Habit #21
Learn How to Apologize Mindfully

There is a popular saying from the Erich Segal novel *Love Story* (and 1970 movie by the same name); one of the main characters, Jennifer, says to her lover, Oliver, "Love means never having to say you're sorry."

It's true that in a mindful relationship you shouldn't have to apologize for who you are and what you feel. Each partner should have a compassionate acceptance of the other, even when he or she makes mistakes.

But love also means taking full responsibility for your actions and the impact they have on the one you love. As much as we accept our beloved and are willing to forgive and forget many things, there are times when an apology must be offered before healing can begin.

Studies reinforce that love does indeed mean having to say you're sorry. Apologizing and asking for forgiveness is one of the most significant factors contributing to relationship satisfaction. Being able to move on from hurtful, negative events will ultimately lead to a stronger connection.

Couples who learn to offer sincere apologies to each other can expunge the toxic hurt and shame that prevents them from having emotional intimacy. However, apologizing is an advanced relationship skill, one that calls for attentive commitment.

It requires doing something most of us find extremely difficult—getting past the ego self. Many people simply can't apologize, or they do so flippantly or with resistance. The fear of admitting weakness or imperfection is too daunting.

The mental process leading to an apology is complex and involves pushing past many internal barriers. We have to honestly examine ourselves and our behavior, the motivation behind the behavior, and the feelings of our partner whom we've injured or offended.

We also need to project into the future to consider the long-term consequences of our actions, a thought process that can be quite uncomfortable.

Simply acknowledging we've messed up is the place most people get stuck. The minute we acknowledge this, we're in a vulnerable position. We aren't the strong, flawless, competent person we want to project to our spouse or partner. As soon as we admit to ourselves we've done something wrong, we feel diminished and lose some amount of self-esteem.

This self-esteem can be restored through apology, but our knee-jerk reaction is believing we are stronger by refusing to admit our mistake. We defend our actions, point fingers, or deflect the impact our behavior has had. We tell ourselves our words or actions were justified or necessary.

We can really dig in if our partner reacts with anger or extreme emotion. Things begin to escalate, and now you have another buffer of emotional intensity keeping you from self-honesty. But have you noticed how blaming others never makes you feel better?

In fact, the only true way to get past certain conflicts is by fully admitting your mistake and apologizing sincerely. Only then can you move forward with peace and confidence to restore your integrity and repair the relationship.

How to Develop This Habit

Be honest with yourself—are you prideful and resistant when it comes to owning your mistakes and saying, "I'm sorry," right away?

If you have a hard time apologizing (or you don't apologize in a timely way), this is an important habit to prioritize. Don't allow a backlog of hurt feelings and resentments to erode your partner's love and respect for you.

Do you have something tugging at your heart right now that requires an apology? If so, a good way to practice this habit is by making a sincere and complete apology to your partner right away, using the skills outlined here.

On an ongoing basis, you'll need to remain vigilant about any tendencies to be defensive or resistant when it comes to apologizing. Use a visual reminder to help you keep this habit top of mind, though your partner will likely let you know when you've done something that requires an apology. Your goal is to offer it before he or she has to ask for one.

Remember—acknowledging your mistakes, apologizing, asking forgiveness, and correcting behavior aren't signs of weakness. They are signs of emotional maturity.

Pay attention to your feelings.

We often know we've said or done something wrong the minute it happens. We feel that queasy, oops-I-messed-up feeling inside. Most of us want to push that feeling aside, but the sooner you address a mistake the better.

When you ignore the feeling, you're only delaying the inevitable—and you make yourself look insensitive. If you *feel* you've done something wrong, then you probably have, even if your partner hasn't called you out on it. Be honest with yourself about why you're experiencing the feeling and what you did wrong.

It can help to step outside of your own ego and pretend you are the recipient of the words or behavior that prompted your discomfort. Would you want an apology from yourself?

Pay attention to your partner's reactions.

Sometimes the first cue that you've hurt the one you love comes from your partner. He or she may tell you directly with calm or angry words, or your partner might show you passively by withdrawing or behaving differently toward you.

Sometimes when your partner is wounded, he or she may have a harder time expressing intense emotions. There's often resentment involved, and the longer you're detached from your partner's pain, the worse it gets.

If you suspect you've hurt your beloved, and you notice a difference in behavior, or if he or she tells you directly, then pay attention. Even if you believe in the moment that you aren't in the wrong, acknowledge your partner's pain. Take your partner's hands, look him or her in the eye, and say, "I see that I've hurt you, and I didn't mean to do that."

Try to step into his or her shoes and practice empathy. Just listening and acknowledging in a calm and receptive way can defuse a painful, emotionally charged situation.

Reflect on your actions and investigate them further.

When you are calm and not feeling defensive or angry, reflect honestly on your actions and how they hurt your partner. You'll likely come up with many reasons why you behaved as you did, and perhaps you have some legitimate rationalizations. But if there is any part of your behavior that was wrong, you must accept responsibility.

If you aren't sure, or your feelings are getting in the way of self-honesty, find someone you trust who can give you some balanced feedback on the situation.

There are some situations when you are clearly and completely in the wrong, and other times it's not so black and white. But if some aspect of your behavior was wrong, an apology for your part is still in order.

Be sure to act quickly.

As soon as you know you need to apologize, do it quickly. Allow emotions to calm down, and take the time for reflection if necessary. But after that, it's time to take a deep breath and make amends.

Any offense seems worse over time. It can grow out of proportion and cause deeper hurt as your partner has more time to ponder it and live with the pain.

The longer you wait, the more difficult it will be for you to step forward and accept responsibility for your actions. Make apologizing your priority once you know it needs to happen.

Make your apology in person.

A complete apology should be offered face to face (not by text or email) and involves four parts:

1. Sit down with your partner, look him or her in the eye, and acknowledge your wrongdoing.

2. Say you are sorry for your actions. Use the words, "I'm sorry," and "I was wrong."

3. Ask for forgiveness.

4. Promise to do better going forward.

"Sweetheart, I really messed up by forgetting the dinner party. I know how much it meant to you, and I am deeply sorry. I hope you'll forgive me. I promise to be more attentive and organized next time."

If your partner is still angry and expresses anger and pain, listen and acknowledge them. Show humility and real sorrow for your actions.

Don't try to defend your actions or make excuses. Don't try to deflect blame onto anyone else. When you are apologizing for *your* behavior, take complete and full ownership of your mistake.

Don't dilute it.

You may feel your partner is partly culpable or has something he needs to apologize for as well. This may be true, but your moment of apology isn't the time to expect one from him.

Offer your apology unconditionally, and don't get offended or defensive if an apology isn't forthcoming from your partner. Apologizing can soften the heart of your partner, and he or she might spontaneously say "I'm sorry" as well. But if that doesn't happen, simply accept his or her response graciously.

Then later, if you wish to bring up your feelings about your partner's behavior, do so without attaching it to your apology. Tell her how her behavior impacted you, but don't demand a reciprocal mea culpa.

Your apology needs to come from a legitimate feeling of remorse related to your behavior—even if you never get an apology in return.

Apologize again if necessary.

Some mistakes require more than one apology. If you've really broken your partner's trust, have repeatedly crossed boundaries, or intentionally embarrassed or hurt them, you've got some ground to cover before the relationship can be healed.

You may need to acknowledge your wrongdoing several times and apologize repeatedly until the other person feels and accepts your sincerity. This is especially necessary when your spouse experiences ongoing pain, distrust, and grief as a result of your actions.

Don't stop with a verbal apology.

If you want to heal the relationship and regain trust, you will need to go further than a verbal apology alone. You must change your behavior and take any specific actions needed to make your partner feel secure in your integrity.

If your offense was deeply wounding, you may need to go above and beyond ordinary measures to make him or her feel confident in you again. For example, if you had a marital affair or spent a huge sum of money without your partner's knowledge, you may need to be overly transparent about your behaviors for many months.

Words are important, but they are empty if you don't commit to doing better in the future. Show your partner that you are truly sorry and that you fully intend to change your ways.

Admitting your mistake, taking ownership of it, and sincerely apologizing is never easy. However, it's inevitable that you will be in this position many times in your relationship.

Having the courage and emotional maturity to make a complete and sincere apology will strengthen your connection, boost your partner's respect for you, and bolster your own self-esteem.

Mindful Relationship Habit #22
Spice Up Your Sex Life

We probably don't need to tell you this, but sex is good for your relationship. A number of studies reinforce the obvious: the more sex you and your partner have, the higher your relationship satisfaction, regardless of your age. Having sex once a week is enough to give you a lingering happiness surge and keep you close as a couple.

In addition to making you happier and closer as a couple, sex has so many physical and emotional benefits that you may want to stop reading and just go have sex right now. Or wait 30 seconds and read the benefits below first.

According to science, an active sex life:

- » increases level of commitment and emotional intimacy
- » boosts self-esteem and makes you feel younger
- » lowers the level of the stress hormone cortisol
- » lowers feelings of insecurity
- » reinforces a more positive attitude
- » makes you calmer and less irritable
- » relieves stress and reduces depression
- » reduces the risk of physical illness

» improves immunity and helps prevent colds and flu

» reduces pain by increasing endorphins

» improves overall fitness and burns about 200 calories (per 30 minutes of active sex)

» lowers mortality rates

» reduces the risk of prostate cancer

» improves posture

» reduces risk of heart disease

» helps prevent yeast infections

» lightens menstrual periods and cramps

» firms stomach and buttocks

» lowers blood pressure

» improves sleep

» improves digestion

» improves sense of smell

» improves bladder control

» promotes healthier teeth

» increases DHEA hormone, which makes your skin healthier

» increases circulation

» improves memory

» produces brain chemicals to stimulate the growth of new dendrites

» improves pelvic muscle tone

» boosts libido

Remember the early days of your relationship when having amazing, mind-blowing sex wasn't something you worried about? You didn't need to be reminded of the benefits—sex happened spontaneously and with wild abandon.

Now you have a few years under your belts together (pun intended), and perhaps the sex is less frequent and less novel. If this is true for you, you aren't alone. Fully one-third of Americans 18 to 59 have sex less than once a month according to research. So what has happened over the years to throw cold water on your sex life?

For most couples, just the passion-sapping demands of modern life are enough to make your libidos limp. The time and effort involved in your careers, household chores, childrearing, and life obligations can drain you of energy. By the end of the day, one or both of you is so exhausted that sex feels more like a chore than a pleasure.

Hormonal changes, loss of desire, pornography, unresolved conflict, alcohol or drug use, and awkwardness initiating sexual encounters all can contribute to less-than-satisfying physical intimacy.

Another barrier to a healthy physical relationship is the discomfort many of us have communicating our sexual needs. Sex can be one of the most difficult topics to discuss due to embarrassment or fear of rejection. But a breakdown in communication about sex can result in some unfortunate and serious consequences for your relationship.

If you saw the movie *Hope Springs*, about a middle-aged couple whose marriage is unraveling, you can see how the inability to be open and honest about sex leads to a sad and slow drifting apart where the couple lives more like distant roommates than lovers.

Even the closest of couples have trouble talking openly and honestly about sex. Canadian researcher E. Sandra Byers found that rates of discussing sexual needs with an intimate partner, even in committed long-term relationships, were surprisingly low.

Maybe it's because we know that anything we reveal about our sexual needs and desires has the potential to scare, offend, and unsettle our partner. We fear that saying the wrong thing about our own sexual tastes or assumptions might expose us as foolish, ignorant, or even depraved.

However, in the face of any discomfort, embarrassment, and anxiety— you need to be able to say, "I like this, I prefer this over that, I fantasize about this." You need to find each other's bodies familiar and comfortable territory that you explore without shame or embarrassment.

You also need to be able to discuss why there might be a loss of interest and frequency in sex or why there might be a performance issue. According to many experts, a loss of sexual desire is often a symptom of deeper issues in the relationship, like a breakdown in communication in general. Unraveling issues with your sex life can help you address these other problems if you both remain open to exploring your emotions.

There are so many compelling reasons to be having sex regularly. So don't allow this vital part of your relationship to fizzle out or limp along on autopilot. Of all the habits you can practice as a couple, this one has the most potential for fun and pleasure!

How to Develop This Habit

Hopefully, you're convinced that communicating about sex is necessary in order to improve your physical intimacy and make it more exciting. Knowing this is true, you have to make time to discuss it.

If you haven't talked about sex much in the past, you may need one initial conversation to discuss your current feelings about your sex life in general. Discuss your discomfort with talking about sex and try to be more open about your attitudes and beliefs about sex.

During this conversation, schedule a regular time to talk about your sex life and each other's needs, desires, and fantasies. Maybe it's once a week or once a month, but put it on the calendar until you both get more comfortable naturally initiating the conversation.

Be sure you talk in a space that is comfortable and free of distractions and interruptions. Also, make sure you talk when you are both in a good frame of mind, rather than choosing a time when you're tired or irritated.

To help you with this conversation, answer the following questions about your sexual relationship with your spouse or partner. For any item in which you answered "somewhat true" or "not true," make notes about why you don't feel the statement is true for you.

Discuss your answers and comments with your partner and identify areas you both feel you need to improve. Devise a plan for having regular conversations about your sexual intimacy and the efforts you are making together.

Here are 17 statements you could consider:

1. In general, I am satisfied with our sexual relationship.

___Very true   ___Mostly true   ___Somewhat true   ___Not true

2. I am happy with the frequency of sex between us.

___Very true   ___Mostly true   ___Somewhat true   ___Not true

3. I am happy with the amount and kind of foreplay before sex.

___Very true   ___Mostly true   ___Somewhat true   ___Not true

4. I am happy with the amount of nonsexual touch and affection with my partner.

___Very true   ___Mostly true   ___Somewhat true   ___Not true

5. I feel my partner and I have the same level of sexual desire.

___Very true   ___Mostly true   ___Somewhat true   ___Not true

6. I feel safe and comfortable initiating sex with my partner.

___Very true   ___Mostly true   ___Somewhat true   ___Not true

7. I feel safe and comfortable turning down sex with my partner.

___Very true   ___Mostly true   ___Somewhat true   ___Not true

8. I feel safe and secure when my partner turns down sex with me.

___Very true   ___Mostly true   ___Somewhat true   ___Not true

9. I feel desired by my partner.

___Very true   ___Mostly true   ___Somewhat true   ___Not true

10. I feel comfortable telling my partner my sexual desires or fantasies.

___Very true   ___Mostly true   ___Somewhat true   ___Not true

11. My partner knows what turns me on sexually.

___Very true   ___Mostly true   ___Somewhat true   ___Not true

12. I feel like we can work through our sexual differences and find compromise.

___Very true   ___Mostly true   ___Somewhat true   ___Not true

13. I feel emotionally connected to my partner during sex.

___Very true   ___Mostly true   ___Somewhat true   ___Not true

14. I feel completely at ease during sexual encounters with my partner.

___Very true   ___Mostly true   ___Somewhat true   ___Not true

15. I am in touch with my own sexual needs.

___Very true   ___Mostly true   ___Somewhat true   ___Not true

16. I am comfortable with my body and desirability.

___Very true   ___Mostly true   ___Somewhat true   ___Not true

17. I am comfortable talking with my partner about our sex life.

___Very true   ___Mostly true   ___Somewhat true   ___Not true

Also, here are some questions to help you clarify and communicate your sexual needs:

» What might make talking about sex with your partner more comfortable?

» How often would you and your partner like to have conversations about your sex life together? Daily? Weekly? Monthly?

» What is one sexual fantasy you'd like to share with your partner?

> » What are your sexual boundaries? Are there sexual activities you won't participate in?

> » What are three things you find sexually attractive about your partner?

> » If you have lost sexual desire, or if your sex life has taken a nosedive, what do you think is the bigger issue behind this problem?

> » What do you think needs to happen to address this bigger issue?

Be positive and gentle with your words.

We all feel vulnerable about our sexual attractiveness, and the last thing you want to do is criticize or shame your partner. As you discuss your answers to the previous questions, remember your goal is to improve your sex life and your intimacy as a couple.

Frame all of your concerns, desires, and needs in positive and loving language. So rather than saying, "You never kiss me during lovemaking," say something like, "I love the way you kiss and would really like more kissing when we make love."

As the old saying goes, "You catch more flies with honey than vinegar," and the same holds true with your partner. Reinforce what you like, and ask for something different in a kind and gentle way. Don't say, "I don't like when you touch me there," but say something like, "Can we explore touching me in different places during foreplay?"

Talk through differing sexual needs and how to reach compromise.

We all have different preferences about how often we want sex, what time of day and where we want it, how much foreplay we need, how much nonsexual touch we need before sex, and how much cuddling we need after sex.

Men and women tend to be different in these needs, and these differences can lead to conflict and frustration if they aren't addressed. Be open with one another about your differing needs, and then talk about how to resolve these differences through compromise and negotiation.

Devise a ritual for initiating sex that works for both of you. Maybe it's as straightforward as saying, "I want to make love." Or it could be a physical gesture or a written invitation.

More importantly, find a way to refuse a sexual encounter that doesn't make your partner feel rejected or unattractive. If you are totally not in the mood, then say something like, "I love making love to you, and you are so sexy, but right now I'm really not in the mood. Can I take a rain check?"

As you get more comfortable talking about sex, discuss your fantasies or specific sexual desires.

It may be hard to look your partner in the eye and tell him or her your secret desire to have sex while tied to the bedpost or to explain in graphic detail exactly where you want to be stimulated and how. But having these conversations can definitely spice up your sex life and empower your partner to please you in ways he or she may not have considered.

If you can't verbalize these fantasies at first, write them down and share them with your partner that way. Just discussing your fantasies, whether or not you act them out, can be a form of foreplay and intimacy.

If you are both game for whatever is brought forward, that's great. But there may be times when one of you doesn't feel comfortable with a fantasy of the other. You need to respect your partner's boundaries without pressuring him or her, just as you should be able to share your fantasies without your partner shaming or judging you.

Make sex a priority.

If your lives are so busy that you can't seem to find time for sex, or you always feel too exhausted, you need to address these issues first. If you value sexual intimacy as an important part of your relationship, you need to prioritize it.

One way to do this is by scheduling a day and time for sex, just as you set aside time for meals and other activities. This may not feel very romantic or spontaneous, but it ensures that sex happens and doesn't get pushed aside in favor of the latest Netflix series or football game.

Set a time for sex when you know you won't be stressed, overly tired, or potentially interrupted by kids or anyone else. Hire a babysitter to take the kids out of the house if necessary. Try to keep the hours before making love calm and free of conflict so you don't have any lingering irritations between you.

Develop a special ritual around your encounters with candles, music, lingerie, and lotions. Or surprise one another with something different—a fantasy acted out, a long sexy shower together, using toys, or even a heated quickie.

Advance your sex education.

Couples often get stuck in a rut with their sexual encounters. They begin the same way, they happen in the same room, and they unfold with the same positions and mechanics. When there's little creativity and novelty, sex becomes mundane.

You may need some inspiration and even education to spice up your physical encounters. There are hundreds of books, videos, and toys you can purchase at the touch of a button (and in the privacy of your home) to enlighten you on new ways to explore and expand your sexual encounters.

Try to view this experimentation as a way to enhance your overall intimacy—not just as a way to achieve a better orgasm. Allow your sexual encounters to be close and pleasurable rituals from beginning to end where you aren't trying to achieve anything except to connect and explore each other's bodies.

Divide chores equally for better sex.

Yes, you read that correctly. Dividing your chores is the new aphrodisiac. A recent study shows that when partners feel there is a more equal division of household chores, sexual intimacy improves.

"Feelings of fairness and satisfaction with the division of housework are central to couples' relationship satisfaction, which is strongly related to sexual intimacy," says the authors of the study, Daniel L. Carlson, Amanda J. Miller, Sharon Sassler, and Sarah Hanson.

If one partner is handling more of the load, he or she will begin to feel resentful and overwhelmed, emotions that don't inspire romantic desire.

If you want to improve your sex life, work together to negotiate a fair and equal division of labor around the house and with child-rearing, based on your work schedules and other obligations.

Talk about the issues that may be behind a lack of desire.

If your sex life has taken a nosedive, and it's lasted for a while, there might be a deeper emotional reason. It could be that you are angry or you feel wounded by your partner. Maybe you feel insecure about your attractiveness or desirability. There might be something about your partner (like weight gain, for example) making him or her less desirable to you.

Some of these issues are less emotionally charged than others. Saying, "I don't feel like making love until we work through last week's argument," is a lot easier to express than, "I don't feel like making love because you've gained so much weight."

But unless these issues are addressed, they will fester and slowly erode your close bond. If there's a problem related to sex or your sexual desire that you fear might wound your partner or that you're afraid to address, then go meet with a relationship counselor together. A trained counselor can help you navigate the situation and find solutions. Don't let discomfort or anxiety keep you from having a satisfying sexual relationship.

Mindful Relationship Habit #23
Practice Playfulness

Do you and your partner have fun together every day? Do you feel lighthearted and playful around each other more often than not? Can you still be silly, make each other laugh, and find humor in the challenges you face together?

Cultivating the practice of playfulness as a couple is more important to your relationship happiness than you might imagine. Research underscores that playfulness plays a vital role in creating long-lasting relationships, and it "helps couples to overcome routine difficulties, prevents boredom, and boosts positive emotions."

So what exactly is playfulness in an adult relationship? It is, in part, returning to a childlike mind-set that frees you to enjoy life with your partner. It is an energy of lightness and joie de vivre that runs through your relationship.

In her paper *Playfulness, "World"-Travelling, and Loving Perception*, Maria Lugones eloquently describes what playfulness is in a love relationship:

> *Playfulness is, in part, an openness to being a fool, which is a combination of not worrying about competence, not being self-important, not taking norms as sacred and finding ambiguity and double edges a source of wisdom and delight.*

So, positively, the playful attitude involves openness to surprise, openness to being a fool, openness to self-construction or reconstruction and to construction or reconstruction of the "worlds" we inhabit playfully. Negatively, playfulness is characterized by uncertainty, lack of self-importance, absence of rules or a not taking rules as scared, a no worrying about competence and a lack of abandonment to a particular construction of oneself, others and one's relation to them.

You may remember being more playful at the beginning of your relationship with your partner. You could tease each other, act silly, flirt, and laugh together easily. Perhaps you made up fun games or rituals that were shared just between the two of you.

You chased each other, tickled, made faces, or did crazy dances together. You could even be playful in bed with your sexual intimacy. The two of you just had fun together—an intimate, liberating, intensely shared kind of fun.

As time goes on in a marriage or long-term relationship, our lives become more complicated and often very serious. We are involved in the serious business of grown-up couple stuff. We work hard. We support our families. We worry about money and higher prices. We fret about the condition of the world, politics, or our children. We have endless chores and tasks without much time for fun.

We lose our sense of playfulness due to stress, overwhelm, frustration, exhaustion, and perhaps a sense that having fun is an indulgence we can no longer afford. All that seriousness and stress can take a toll on your relationship. It can make it feel like a business arrangement. It can take the wind out of your sails.

In this environment, it's easy to forget about playfulness and how important it is to your connection as a couple. Perhaps it's been too long since fun lived with you every day as a regular companion. Fun may not come knocking at your door, so you may have to invite it in. You have to make playfulness a habit, learn it as a skill, and make time for it in your lives.

You don't need to feel guilty or embarrassed about being playful together. Being an adult doesn't mean you've lost the childlike quality of wonder and joy and wild abandonment. It's only as we age that *real fun* is abandoned. Playfulness doesn't need to be structured or competitive. It is more a relaxed state of mind that leads to moments of mutual joy and easy vulnerability.

It's okay to be goofy and unabashedly happy together sometimes. Let your hair fly in the wind. Lighten up about the serious business of being adults, and open the door to more playfulness and fun in your lives together.

How to Develop This Habit

Developing the habit of playfulness is one that you can mindfully practice daily. Although you eventually want playfulness to be a natural, spontaneous way of interacting together, setting a day and time to practice it is a great way to reintroduce it into your daily lives.

Consider practicing this habit every day at the same time of day for four to six weeks. Choose a time when you are relatively relaxed and can set aside 15–20 minutes for fun and playfulness. If you have children, you may be tempted to include them in your playtime, but remember this is a time for reconnecting as a couple.

If you and your partner haven't been playful with each other in a while, this habit work may feel awkward and uncomfortable at first. Just stick with it, and you will eventually loosen up and enjoy this new freedom to be childlike again.

Remember your early playful times.

Begin this habit by reflecting together on your early relationship days and how you were playful back then. Talk about the silly things you did together, the ways you had fun and enjoyed just being around each other in a light and happy way.

Talk about specific memories with as much detail as you can remember. As you discuss these memories, make notes about any activities or moments that you might want to revive as you work on this habit.

Brainstorm ideas for playfulness.

Prepare for your playfulness practice sessions by coming up with a list of ideas for having fun and being playful for 15–20 minutes (or longer, if you have the time). Be sure whatever you include isn't competitive but rather cooperative.

Be creative and humorous with the ideas you develop, and enjoy the time together brainstorming. This is an opportunity for playfulness in itself!

Here are a number of ideas to get you started:

- » Get some bubble soap and wands and blow bubbles together.
- » Go outside and climb a tree.
- » Lie down outside and count stars or identify cloud shapes.

» Put on rock music and dance.

» Have a scavenger hunt around the house.

» Write each other silly love poems.

» Talk to each other in "Pig Latin."

» Wash each other's hair in the sink.

» Paint each other's toenails.

» Rake up a big leaf pile and jump in together.

» Read out loud to each other in foreign accents.

» Draw pictures of your favorite sexual positions together.

» Build an indoor fort.

» Play in the sprinkler on a warm day.

» Have a Nerf gun war.

» Look at baby pictures of each other.

» Play strip poker (which might lead to more fun).

» Do something totally unexpected and silly.

» Play the game Twister.

» Go outside and play catch.

» Tie your legs together and complete your dinner preparations this way.

» Create your bucket list together.

» Take a walk—and hold hands and skip for part of it.

» Plan a surprise for each other.

» Take a walk together in the pouring rain.

» Wrap each other up in toilet paper and take pictures.

» Paint a picture together.

» Play the block-stacking game of Jenga together.

» Have a quickie in an unexpected place wearing all of your clothes (except the essential ones).

Extend your playfulness to date nights.

Date nights are surprisingly important to the health of your relationship and provide more opportunities for playfulness. According to a study by the Marriage Foundation, couples that have a monthly date night are 14% less likely to break up.

Another recent study by The National Marriage Project called "The Date Night Opportunity" confirmed that date nights foster stronger relationships and marriages. Date night adds excitement and novelty to the connection, which leads to more satisfaction in the relationship.

As you add playfulness to your daily life, remember to extend it with longer date nights that involve fun and playfulness. Set up weekly dates, and try to do something where you are active and engaged with one another, rather than falling back on the typical dinner-and-a-movie date.

Going bike riding, hiking, bowling, dancing, taking a cooking class, going on a picnic, attending an outdoor festival, or taking a sunset motorcycle ride are ideas that are worth exploring. If you get stuck, here are 50 creative ideas you can use to plan your next date night.

Use playfulness in your daily tasks and interactions.

You can reduce some of the stress that shuts down playfulness by being more lighthearted and playful with your daily tasks and life obligations.

Pop your spouse playfully with the dish towel. Give him a quick spray with the garden hose. Make a suggestive comment as she's leaning over the bed to make it up.

You can also "gamify" some of your chores by doing them together and applying a special challenge or quirky rules or by setting a timer to see who can finish first. Turn on some music while you clean, and just enjoy being partners who work and play together.

In the evening, rather than surfing your computers or turning on the evening news, cook dinner together while listening to music and enjoying a glass of wine. Parent together in a more playful and cooperative way, showing your kids teamwork and humor even when they challenge you.

Try hard to remember that life is short. It is meant to be enjoyed and experienced fully. Try to catch yourself when you see you are getting overly stressed and serious and look for the humor in difficult or unpleasant situations that arise throughout the day.

Address bigger issues that impact playfulness.

Life does present us with serious challenges and stressors that impact our emotional health. These life events can make us brittle and anxious, unable to respond to our partner's efforts at playfulness or to initiate any ourselves. Having fun seems like an impossible indulgence when life is so stressful.

Often, we take on too much, spend more than we should, or neglect to manage our lives in ways that help us stay centered and lighthearted. All of the stress can make us grouchy, angry, fretful, and distant. But this is not what your partner deserves, and it certainly doesn't help your own physical or mental health.

You owe it to yourself and your partner to deal with whatever it is that's preventing you from enjoying life and each other. This might mean changing jobs, cutting back on spending, finally dealing with an ongoing challenge, or saying no to some obligations. Do what needs to be done to reduce your stress so you can find joy again in your relationship.

Mindful Relationship Habit #24
Disconnect from Digital Devices

The impact of our digital devices can be viewed as the 21st century relationship challenge, one that our parents and grandparents didn't have to contend with in their marriages. They weren't lured away from each other by this infinite vortex of virtual distraction. They certainly had other distractions, but none so insidious and harmful to real intimacy as our digital devices have become.

It all happened so fast. We didn't have the time to set healthy boundaries for smartphone usage, and now we find them as the uninvited third wheel in our romantic relationships. Consider the couples you see in restaurants that, instead of talking or engaging have their heads down and thumbs flipping through apps or snapping pictures of their food to share on Instagram.

We compulsively carry our smartphones with us wherever we go—the office, the bathroom, the outdoors. Our phone is always in hand, as if it were some magical connection to a world that is far more exciting and real than the reality we are living.

The Internet is even putting up a barrier between couples in the inner sanctum of the bedroom. It seems the once-sacred time in bed we spent talking, cuddling, and winding down together is now used for endless solo scrolling with our backs to each other.

Of course, smartphones are useful in many circumstances and make our lives easier. However, they infect our relationships in devious ways with an almost addictive attraction. One of the most unfortunate consequences of our tech-tethered lives is that we are no longer fully present with our partners.

We unconsciously replace real-life interactions with virtual experiences, until we find it nearly impossible to wholeheartedly devote our attention to the present moment. As a result, we lose many moments of engagement with our partners that are unique and never to be lived again.

Smartphones can also be the culprit of communication breakdown between couples. Intimacy is hard to achieve or maintain when your phone keeps beeping with alerts, notifications, and email reminders. A constant, merciless distraction, smartphones sabotage the deeply felt, long conversations that strengthen the bonds between you.

In fact, some people talk more about their relationships on social media than they do face to face with the person they're actually in a relationship with! We become obsessed with how our lives look to others through the digital lens and forget how significant it is to live, invest, and relish the present moment with the person we love.

Excessive smartphone use puts a barrier between couples, making communication more impersonal and shallow. Bonding and intimacy pale in comparison to the lure of instant digital gratification, making it difficult for our relationship to grow and evolve over time.

Overuse of your digital devices also destabilizes your relationship. In order to thrive, a relationship needs to be based on constant give and take, where we consider our partner and his or her needs at least as much as we think about ourselves. Smartphones upset this balance.

They can turn us into self-focused approval-seekers who are too concerned with how many "likes" and retweets we receive. We place too much emphasis on our digital lives and lose sight of the urgency and beauty of the everyday and the person we are most committed to.

Our digital attachments are also a source of relational conflict. You may already get anxious when you can't find your phone or your battery runs low. Maybe you feel irritated when your spouse interrupts your game of *Words with Friends* or suggests you turn your phone off at the dinner table.

The endless access to streaming information and the constant Pavlovian dings and buzzes from our phones keep us on high alert and always "on." This information overload leaves us exhausted and mentally spent, which further separates us from our partners.

Have you and your partner had conflicts related to the amount of time one or the other spends on digital devices? Has one of you felt like the other is checked out or constantly distracted? As if we don't have enough to contend with in modern life, these digital devices have created unnecessary reasons for arguments, stress, and detachment.

Dropping our bad habits with our devices requires a big mental shift. We shouldn't feel stressed and anxious when we're in phone-free zones. We should be relieved—relieved that we can cherish the special moments happening each day and spend more real time with our partners in the now, which will never be repeated.

Although it's impossible in this day and age to completely give up your digital devices, you need to recognize the profound negative impact they are having on your ability to engage with your partner. How much time are you giving away to virtual reality, only to look up from your phone one day and realize you are living with a stranger?

Don't allow a device of convenience to conveniently erode your intimacy. Make a proactive decision about what role your devices will play in your relationship going forward, and agree to set boundaries around how much time you will give to these devices when you are together.

How to Develop This Habit

Most of us don't really have a handle on how much time we spend attached to our smartphones or other digital devices. They have become such an integral part of our lives that we rarely leave home (or the room) without them. You may not be aware of how significantly your tech dependency is impacting the quality and intimacy of your relationship.

The best way to know whether or not this is a habit you need to work on is by honestly assessing your current digital device habits. Answer the following questions to help you get a better idea.

How many hours a day do you spend on your smartphone, tablet, or computer for non-work-related activities?

___Less than an hour

___One to three hours

___Three to five hours

___More than five hours

When you are using your digital devices, how much of that time happens when you are with your spouse or partner?

___None of it

___A little of it

___Much of it

___Most of it

Do you frequently wish your partner would put down his or her phone or shut down other devices and engage with you instead?

Do you or your partner spend more than an hour a day on social media (unrelated to work)?

How do you think your time (and your partner's time) spent on your digital devices has impacted your communication and connection as a couple? Make notes about this, citing specific examples if possible.

Define digital device boundaries in your relationship.

Now that you have a better idea about the amount of time you spend on your devices and how it's impacting your relationship, sit down together to discuss your boundaries around the use of these devices going forward. Consider which of the following boundaries you want to implement:

» No devices allowed while dining together (at home or out).

» No devices allowed when you are in bed together.

» No devices allowed in the bedroom altogether.

» No devices allowed when you are having a serious discussion or resolving conflict.

» No devices allowed when you first wake up for at least 30 minutes.

» No devices allowed when you first see each other at the end of the workday for at least 30 minutes.

» No devices allowed when you go on fun outings together.

» No devices or limited device usage when you are on vacation.

» No devices allowed when you have family meetings.

» No devices allowed when you are entertaining at home.

» No using devices when one partner is trying to talk to the other.

» No devices on special holidays or occasions (i.e., Christmas Day, Sundays, etc.).

Add additional rules and boundaries you'd like to make around using digital devices if you don't see them in this list.

Replace your bad habits with positive ones.

Dropping your habits around your digital devices will be difficult. These devices reinforce your addiction to them by providing a constant source of gratification and connection with the outside world. Because they are so ubiquitous in our culture, you feel "lesser than" and out of touch if you aren't plugged in. You will need to be diligent and committed to your efforts if you want to cut back.

Part of successfully dropping a bad habit is replacing it with a new positive behavior. The goal here is to use this time more mindfully with your partner. As you review each of the new boundaries you have established around your devices, you'll need to be very specific about what you will and won't do with your devices and what you will do instead of engaging with them.

The easiest way to prevent yourself from using your devices is by turning them off and putting them out of sight. For example, leave them at home when you go out to dinner, or put them in another room before bed.

However, we often feel it's necessary to have our phones available "in case of emergency."

If you have children who may need to reach you, or if you use your phone for business, it may be unwise to check out completely. You'll need to figure out how often you can check your phone and whether you can silence it for each situation. For these brief check-ins, don't allow yourself to get pulled in by news reports, social media alerts, or texts.

Start small.

We suggest you begin by working on just one of the boundaries you've set around your devices—maybe one that occurs every day, like no phones in bed. This habit is relatively easy because your phone will be off at a time when you generally aren't needed by other people.

Use the moment you get into bed as a trigger to turn your phones on silent and put them away. Decide how you want to spend your time in bed before sleep, hopefully by cuddling and talking with each other, sharing the events of your day, and asking each other questions. Create new rituals around bedtime that don't involve any devices.

If you read on your phone before bed, you may want to switch to a print book while you are "detoxing" from having your phone in the bed with you so you aren't tempted to scroll around.

Add new digital restrictions and replacement behaviors.

Once you feel you have successfully committed to the first habit change, work on another one. Try something a bit harder, like putting away your devices for 30 minutes to an hour at the end of the workday or in the evening so you can do something together as a couple.

Have a specific plan for how you want to spend this time together that allows you to reconnect, be playful, and enjoy interacting. Don't use television or other distractions as a substitute for your digital time. Focus this time on each other.

You could:

- » take walks
- » go biking together
- » cook dinner together
- » sit outside and talk
- » make love
- » listen to music
- » give each other massages
- » plan a vacation (but without your devices)

Revisit the list of playful activities in Habit #23 or the list of shared rituals in Habit #9 for more ideas.

Mindful Relationship Habit #25
Learn to Love Yourself

Can you be fully available to your partner when you are uncomfortable in your own skin? Is your reservoir of love full enough to offer it unreservedly when your own self-love tank is running on fumes? Do you believe you are worthy and deserving of love?

Your ability to be present and mindfully loving to your partner is rooted in your ability to love yourself. If you can't accept yourself, you'll have a hard time accepting your partner. If you can't forgive yourself, then forgiving your spouse will be a challenge. If you can't be empathetic with yourself, then you'll be reticent to show compassion to your partner.

The more contented and happy you are with yourself, the more you have to offer to your partner and the relationship. Love from your partner doesn't make you whole. Two whole people joining together sets the foundation for a strong relationship. If you aren't whole, if you can't love and accept yourself, then developing this ability is essential for your relationship to flourish.

Healthy self-love is an indispensable quality for both partners, as it gives your relationship a sense of ease and flow. When you are comfortable with yourself, the relationship is more comfortable. When you're okay with who you are, you don't look to your partner to make up for your perceived deficiencies. Because you are self-assured, you don't drag down the relationship with jealousy and insecurities.

Loving yourself involves a combination of confidence, self-acceptance, and humility. You know your strengths but can acknowledge and accept your flaws without seeing your essential self as being flawed. You embrace who you are, where you've come from, and how much more you can learn and grow.

You value yourself enough to have healthy boundaries with others, including your partner. You forgive yourself for past mistakes and show self-compassion whenever you fall short of your own expectations. You can enjoy your own company, and you value time alone to reconnect with yourself more deeply.

Your ability to love yourself is a highly attractive quality to your partner and others around you. When you are happy with who you are, you can offer your best, most centered, and most confident self to your partner—and your partner feels free to be authentic and confident with you.

As important as self-love is to our relationships, many of us have a hard time practicing it. We may know in our heads we are worthy, but we don't feel it in our hearts. We don't believe it when our partner says, "You're beautiful, smart, and capable." Instead, we believe that little inner voice whispering, "You're ugly, stupid, and unlovable."

When we don't feel worthy and can't accept our flaws and weaknesses, we either shove down our feelings (which manifests in depression and anxiety), or we express them in unhealthy ways (through anger, passive-aggressive behaviors, or dysfunction). It's hard to be a mindful and caring partner when we are unhappy with ourselves.

Low self-esteem and a lack of self-love can undermine your relationship with a variety of intimacy-sabotaging behaviors that you might recognize:

- » neediness, insecurity, and people-pleasing
- » constant approval seeking
- » jealousy
- » controlling behaviors
- » codependence
- » loss of individuality
- » blaming others
- » defensiveness and hypersensitivity
- » hypervigilance, extreme fear of making mistakes
- » passive-aggressiveness
- » perfectionism
- » poor personal boundaries
- » sexual problems
- » addictions
- » underachievement
- » workaholic behaviors
- » inauthenticity, wearing a mask

Self-love can be difficult because the world doesn't always reflect back to us what we'd like to believe about ourselves. We've forgotten how to trust ourselves and rely on our own beliefs and judgments. Instead, we look to others to build us up and manufacture our self-esteem. If others don't like the person we are, we struggle to become someone else who meets the world's approval instead of affirming our own uniqueness.

As Barrie writes on her blog, Live Bold and Bloom:

> *Here's an insight I've embraced in recent years: life isn't about achieving some outward standard of success, achievement, or physical perfection. It is about becoming more and more of who YOU are. It is about continual self-evolution and authenticity. It is about diving into the depths of your unique self and coming up with treasure after treasure that was previously unknown to you. You are a veritable sunken Titanic of mysteries to be explored.*

To embrace your true worth, you can learn new ways of thinking about yourself and responding to the input you receive from the world around you. You can also pay attention to the behaviors that make a truly happy, healthy connection with your partner more difficult.

Like any other habit, the habit of loving yourself requires self-awareness, practice, and vigilance. Sometimes it requires the support of a professional therapist to help you deal with the deeper causes of low self-esteem that keep you trapped.

We have put this habit last because we believe it is the most important for you and your partner. Loving yourself is your highest calling, your most important work, the most life-changing thing you can ever do for yourself and your relationship.

If you want a mindful relationship that continues to grow and thrive, then continue to work on yourself. Address what is keeping you from savoring the richness of a whole and evolved relationship and from being the kind of partner your partner deserves.

How to Develop This Habit

Most people have times when they don't feel good about themselves or maybe their self-esteem takes a hit. But if a lack of self-love impacts your ability to enjoy life and to have a joyful connection with your spouse or partner, then this is a habit you should prioritize.

Learning to love yourself doesn't happen overnight, especially if you've spent years viewing yourself as "lesser than." You will have to chip away at your old mind-sets and the underlying reasons why you are unhappy with yourself so you can create new, more positive mind-sets and behaviors.

A good way to begin this habit work is to assess how weak or strong your self-love is now. Read the following 26 statements, and write down your answers in your journal or notebook. Make notes about any specific examples you can think of for any of the statements you identified as being "Very true" or "Somewhat true."

1. I tend to focus on my flaws and inadequacies and judge them harshly.

    ___Very True   ___Somewhat True   ___Rarely True

2. I tend to obsess and fixate on everything that's wrong in my life and relationship.

    ___Very True   ___Somewhat True   ___Rarely True

3. I have a hard time forgiving myself for past mistakes.

    ___Very True   ___Somewhat True   ___Rarely True

4. When I fail at something important to me, I become consumed by feelings of inadequacy.

___Very True ___Somewhat True ___Rarely True

5. I am intolerant and impatient toward those aspects of my personality I don't like.

___Very True ___Somewhat True ___Rarely True

6. I tend to feel like most other people are probably happier than I am.

___Very True ___Somewhat True ___Rarely True

7. When something upsets me, my emotions are out of proportion to the situation.

___Very True ___Somewhat True ___Rarely True

8. I am cold-hearted toward myself when I'm experiencing suffering.

___Very True ___Somewhat True ___Rarely True

9. I am not living to my potential because I fear I'm not good enough to succeed.

___Very True ___Somewhat True ___Rarely True

10. I compare myself to others and judge my worthiness by how they appear to me.

___Very True ___Somewhat True ___Rarely True

11. I need a lot of reassurance from my partner and others to feel okay about myself.

___Very True ___Somewhat True ___Rarely True

12. I feel insecure about my partner's love and attraction to me.

___Very True   ___Somewhat True   ___Rarely True

13. I feel jealous that my partner finds others more attractive than me.

___Very True   ___Somewhat True   ___Rarely True

14. I am always worried I'm going to do something wrong.

___Very True   ___Somewhat True   ___Rarely True

15. I feel insecure about my appearance.

___Very True   ___Somewhat True   ___Rarely True

16. I use passive-aggressive ways of telling my partner my needs for fear he or she won't like me if I'm honest.

___Very True   ___Somewhat True   ___Rarely True

17. I need my partner to look or behave a certain way so I can feel good about myself.

___Very True   ___Somewhat True   ___Rarely True

18. I give too much of myself because I don't want to disappoint people.

___Very True   ___Somewhat True   ___Rarely True

19. I tend to pick fights with my partner when I feel bad about myself.

___Very True   ___Somewhat True   ___Rarely True

20. I need everything to be perfect so others won't think I'm inadequate.

___Very True   ___Somewhat True   ___Rarely True

21. I work long hours because I need to prove my worthiness and effectiveness.

    ___Very True   ___Somewhat True   ___Rarely True

22. I don't know the "real" me because I've been pretending to be someone I'm not.

    ___Very True   ___Somewhat True   ___Rarely True

23. It's hard to enjoy sex with my partner because I don't feel good about myself or my body.

    ___Very True   ___Somewhat True   ___Rarely True

24. I drink too much or use drugs to mask the bad feelings I have about myself.

    ___Very True   ___Somewhat True   ___Rarely True

25. I don't take care of my personal needs for rest, self-care, exercise, healthy eating, play, and time off.

    ___Very True   ___Somewhat True   ___Rarely True

26. It is hard for me to be present and attentive with my partner because I'm so focused on my own issues.

    ___Very True   ___Somewhat True   ___Rarely True

After you have completed the assessment for yourself, ask your partner to respond to the statements as they apply to you. Your partner may have a different perspective on your self-esteem and self-love and how it is impacting you as a couple.

Talk about your own answers and the answers your partner gave for you to identify the areas where you are most lacking in love for yourself.

Let's review some habits you can work on to help you foster self-love and improve your relationship by taking responsibility for your own sense of worthiness.

Define worth for yourself.

Can you accept that true worth comes from within? If so, then you need to define what worth means to you. Examine your own values. Define your integrity.

Set aside a quiet time to get clear on what YOU believe, what kind of person you want to be, and how you want to live your life—within the context of what is realistically attainable. Create your own personal operating system for life, without relying on what others think is best for you.

Ask yourself these questions:

» What do I think makes a person worthy?

» What are my values, and am I living in alignment with them?

» What kind of person do I want to be for myself? For my partner?

» In what ways am I living inauthentically, trying to be someone I'm not?

Become aware of your thoughts and challenge them.

Pay attention to the nature of your thoughts and how often you think negative things about yourself. Use a physical reminder, like the rubber band on your wrist, to help you.

Simply cultivating this awareness will allow you to disengage from the thoughts, if only for a few minutes. Diminish the reality and power of your negative thoughts by identifying them. Say something to yourself like, "There are those negative thoughts again. Look at what they are doing to me."

As you become more aware of your thinking patterns, begin to filter your thoughts by applying the light of reality to them. Ask yourself, "Is my thought really the truth? Is it the entire truth or just my perception of the truth?"

Challenge all of your negative thoughts, and seek out evidence that contradicts your negative beliefs. Do what you can to loosen your grasp on self-limiting beliefs that impede your ability to love yourself.

Show compassion for yourself, and practice realistic optimism.

Pretend you are your own best friend, and show the kind of compassion to yourself you would show to someone you care about. Rather than putting yourself down, use words of encouragement and support. You might find this list of 101 positive affirmations useful in working to change your self-talk.

You are as deserving of kindness as anyone, so treat yourself kindly. Don't let your wounded self be the spokesperson for your psyche.

When you really don't believe you're lovable, affirming that you are worthy may feel false. Rather than making blanket statements about your self-worth, identify more honest but optimistic affirmations you can say to yourself.

For example, you might say, "Today I'm not as accomplished as I want to be, but I know I can improve and feel better about myself." Improvement is always possible, and working on an improvement goal will make you feel better about yourself.

Express gratitude daily.

During the times when you catch yourself stuck in negative thinking, switch gears entirely by focusing on gratitude. Make a list of everything you are grateful for in your life—from the most insignificant to the most important. Think about what you are grateful for in yourself and with your partner.

Don't just jot things down quickly. Really focus on each item on the list, and think about how you'd feel without it. Study after study has shown that the regular practice of gratitude helps improve your outlook and feelings of happiness.

You might enjoy this app called Gratitude 365 to keep you on track with gratitude as a daily habit.

Learn the power of acceptance.

Maybe you don't like your face or your body. Maybe you aren't the funniest or most engaging person in your circle. You might look at other people and long to be like them. There are some realities in life that will never change.

Accept what you cannot change about yourself. Everyone has parts of themselves they can't "fix" or alter—aspects of our appearance, personalities, our past experiences, or choices. There are only two options here.

You can forever struggle against those unchangeable things, or you can grow beyond them and choose the path of self-acceptance. The reality that we have these unchangeable things doesn't mean we have to condemn ourselves to a lifetime of unhappiness.

The opportunities for happiness in life are so vast—our flaws are infinitesimal inky droplets in a sea of potential for joyful living. They will dissolve and dissipate if you don't focus on them. By accepting, you free your energy to focus on other more productive, positive endeavors, which will in turn improve your feelings of self-worth.

If positive change is possible, then do whatever you can to change your behaviors, choices, and actions to support your feelings of self-love. Just remember that outward change alone won't make you feel more lovable. You'll feel better about yourself for taking action, but that action must be supported with inner work on your thoughts and beliefs.

Practice self-forgiveness.

To love yourself, you must first forgive yourself and forgive others who have hurt you. You forgive yourself in the same way you forgive a loved one who genuinely seeks forgiveness. You offer it freely and with compassion.

Repeatedly beating yourself up is an exercise in futility.

Feelings of remorse and guilt are natural when you've done something wrong, but they should be used as a motivator for self-correction, not as an eternal whipping post.

Do what needs to be done to right any wrongs and regain your integrity, and then let it go. If others have wounded you, offer the same forgiveness to them—even if they don't seek it. Being able to forgive is a huge step toward self-respect and wholeness.

An excellent mindful practice to help you forgive yourself or someone else is a loving-kindness meditation, as we outlined in Habit #16. Use this meditation to envision compassion for yourself or someone who needs your forgiveness and to reinforce your feelings of forgiveness.

Create an environment that fosters self-love.

If certain environments or situations highlight or reinforce your feelings of low self-worth, change your environment. Put yourself in situations more often where you feel successful, confident, accepted, and happy. Find ways to interact with your partner more often that are lighthearted and fun.

Play to your strengths, and focus on your natural aptitudes rather than struggling against something that constantly brings you down. This might mean changing jobs, finding a hobby or interest that excites you, or setting a goal for achieving something meaningful to you.

If you are surrounded by critical, judgmental people, this will further entrench your feelings of low self-worth. Find supportive friends who are caring, fun, happy, and easy to be around. Let go of people who put you down, try to manipulate you, or treat you poorly. This isn't always easy to do, but letting go of just one negative person can have a huge impact on your day-to-day feelings.

Learn to rely on yourself for approval, rather than your partner.

Remember, two whole individuals coming together to share in life and love is the ideal for a happy, strong relationship. To become whole, you need to take responsibility for your own mental and emotional health.

Of course, you and your partner are there to support one another, but you can't rely on others to constantly prop you up or affirm your self-esteem. Over time, insecurity, neediness, and jealousy will create an imbalance in your relationship and will make your beloved feel more like a caregiver or parent than an equal partner.

If there's something from your childhood or more recent past that has impacted your self-esteem and restricted your ability to love yourself, then take action to heal those wounds. Work with a professional therapist to deal with the root causes of your feelings and to learn strategies for getting stronger and more self-reliant.

Take personal responsibility for loving yourself rather than taking out your feelings of unhappiness, insecurity, or anxiety on your partner.

Learning to love yourself requires patience. If you've spent years disliking or even hating yourself, it will take time to turn the ship around and forge a new direction. You will likely have times of slipping back into old beliefs and negative self-talk. But remember, if you see how the entirety of your life experience hinges on self-love, you will be tenacious and determined to love yourself.

Final Thoughts on *Mindful Relationship Habits*

We'd like to start this final section by *thanking you*. By reading this book all the way to the end, you've demonstrated a commitment to improving the quality of your relationship. Sadly, other couples ignore signs of trouble until it's too late. You on the other hand, have taken that crucial first step toward making a positive change.

As mentioned before, a third to a half of all marriages end in divorce, while 40% of the people are unhappy in their current marriage or relationship. These numbers paint a dismal picture. But even if you're one of these people who currently feels dissatisfied with your relationship, at least you're *doing* something about it.

And speaking of taking action… we encourage you to implement what you've learned. While it would be impossible to implement all 25 habits that we've covered, we recommend **starting with one mindful habit** to share with your partner. This "small win" can lead to series of positive changes throughout all aspects of your relationship.

If you feel stuck with *where* to focus your efforts, then we recommend a simple strategy:

Start by examining your relationship and focusing on the one area causes the most conflict.

Here are a few examples:

If your spouse frequently gets mad because you're not paying attention during a conversation, then you could work on building the practice of active listening (Habit #15).

If you feel like you're not connecting with your loved one on a regular basis, then schedule time to create multiple shared rituals (habit #9).

If you find that your conversations often turn into arguments, then change your communication style. Specifically, you can use "I feel" statements, instead of "you" words when talking to your partner (Habit #17).

If you frequently feel disconnected with your spouse, then schedule a regular meeting where you can talk about your relationship and many of the strategies covered in this book (Habit #1).

And if you realize that you're spending more time on digital devices than with your partner, you can schedule time to purposefully disconnect from technology (Habit #24.)

We all have our blind spots and personal challenges, so it would be impossible to recommend a specific habit as a starting point. Instead, we suggest that you identify your biggest "problem area" and tackle that first. Then, once you have that small win, you can tackle the other positive relationship-building habits that we've covered in this book.

Finally, we want to remind you that acting in a mindful manner in your relationship is a *journey*, not a destination.

Sure, there will be times when you'll be angry or frustrated during conversations. You'll get into the occasional argument. And once in a while, you'll even feel like ending your relationship. But no matter *what* happens, keep focusing on the mindful habits that we've discussed in this book.

Just remember that you're with your partner for a reason. You love this person and chose him or her over anyone else in the world.

Building a more mindful relationship is hard work. In fact, it's a lifelong endeavor. But this work is well worth the effort because being in a great relationship is one of the linchpins to living a life full of happiness and joy.

We wish you the best of luck!

Barrie Davenport & S.J. Scott

One Last Reminder ...

We've covered a wealth of information in this book, but that doesn't mean your self-educational efforts should end here. In fact, we've created a small companion website that includes many resources mentioned throughout *Mindful Relationship Habits*.

So, if you're interested in expanding on what you've learned in this book, then click this link and join us today:

https://www.developgoodhabits.com/mrh-website

Thank You!

Before you go, we'd like to say thank you for purchasing our book.

You could have picked from dozens of books on habit development, but you took a chance and checked out this one.

So, big thanks for downloading this book and reading all the way to the end.

Now we'd like to ask for a small favor. Could you please take a minute or two and leave a review for this book on Amazon?

This feedback will help us continue to write the kind of Kindle books that help you get results. And if you loved it, please let us know.

More Books by Steve

- The Anti-Procrastination Habit: A Simple Guide to Mastering Difficult Tasks

- 10-Minute Mindfulness: 71 Habits for Living in the Present Moment

- Habit Stacking: 127 Small Actions to Improve Your Health, Wealth, and Happiness

- Novice to Expert: 6 Steps to Learn Anything, Increase Your Knowledge, and Master New Skills

- Declutter Your Mind: How to Stop Worrying, Relieve Anxiety, and Eliminate Negative Thinking

- The Miracle Morning for Writers: How to Build a Writing Ritual That Increases Your Impact and Your Income

- 10-Minute Digital Declutter: The Simple Habit to Eliminate Technology Overload

- 10-Minute Declutter: The Stress-Free Habit for Simplifying Your Home

- The Accountability Manifesto: How Accountability Helps You Stick to Goals

- Confident You: An Introvert's Guide to Success in Life and Business

- Exercise Every Day: 32 Tactics for Building the Exercise Habit (Even If You Hate Working Out)

- The Daily Entrepreneur: 33 Success Habits for Small Business Owners, Freelancers and Aspiring 9-to-5 Escape Artists

- Master Evernote: The Unofficial Guide to Organizing Your Life with Evernote (Plus 75 Ideas for Getting Started)

- Bad Habits No More: 25 Steps to Break Any Bad Habit

- Habit Stacking: 97 Small Life Changes That Take Five Minutes or Less

- To-Do List Makeover: A Simple Guide to Getting the Important Things Done

- 23 Anti-Procrastination Habits: Overcome Your Procrastination and Get Results in Your Life

- S.M.A.R.T. Goals Made Simple: 10 Steps to Master Your Personal and Career Goals

- 115 Productivity Apps to Maximize Your Time: Apps for iPhone, iPad, Android, Kindle Fire and PC/iOS Desktop Computers

- Writing Habit Mastery: How to Write 2,000 Words a Day and Forever Cure Writer's Block

- Daily Inbox Zero: 9 Proven Steps to Eliminate Email Overload

- Wake Up Successful: How to Increase Your Energy and Achieve Any Goal with a Morning Routine

- 10,000 Steps Blueprint: The Daily Walking Habit for Healthy Weight Loss and Lifelong Fitness

- 70 Healthy Habits: How to Eat Better, Feel Great, Get More Energy and Live a Healthy Lifestyle

- Resolutions That Stick! How 12 Habits Can Transform Your New Year

More Books by Barrie

- Declutter Your Mind: How to Stop Worrying, Relieve Anxiety, and Eliminate Negative Thinking

- 10-Minute Digital Declutter: The Simple Habit to Eliminate Technology Overload

- 10-Minute Declutter: The Stress-Free Habit for Simplifying Your Home

- 201 Relationship Questions: The Couple's Guide to Building Trust and Emotional Intimacy

- Self-Discovery Questions: 155 Breakthrough Questions to Accelerate Massive Action

- Sticky Habits: 6 Simple Steps to Create Good Habits That Stick

- Finely Tuned: How To Thrive As A Highly Sensitive Person or Empath

- Peace of Mindfulness: Everyday Rituals to Conquer Anxiety and Claim Unlimited Inner Peace

- Confidence Hacks: 99 Small Actions to Massively Boost Your Confidence

- Building Confidence: Get Motivated, Overcome Social Fear, Be Assertive, and Empower Your Life for Success

- The 52-Week Life Passion Project: The Path to Uncover Your Life Passion

43967591R00168